D0416550

Hertfordshire

Almost Ready to Fly

Radio Control Flying 21st Century Style

Almost Ready to Fly

Radio Control Flying 21st Century Style

David Boddington

Special Interest Model Books

Special Interest Model Books Ltd.
P.O. Box 327
Poole
Dorset
BH15 2RG
England

Published by Special Interest Model Books Ltd. 2007

ISBN 978 185486 242 6

www.specialinterestmodelbooks.co.uk

Contents

Chapter 1

Where it Started, Where it's Going

When I started my research for this book what surprised me most was the number of 'Almost Ready to Fly' kits on the market. I knew that 90% of all radio controlled model aircraft kits came into the 'Ready to Fly', or 'Almost Ready to Fly' category, but I hadn't realised that there were quite as many kits on sale, or the number of importers and distributors of these products. As an aeromodeller for many years, both as a hobby and in business. I have watched the gradual decline of the traditional balsawood kit and later, the plastic and veneered foam kits as the 'Almost Ready to Fly' (ARTF) kits became available. There are numerous reasons for the increased popularity in the ARTF kits, it is certainly true that the average hobbyist has less time to pursue their interest than in previous ages or, to put it another way, there are more demands on their spare time than their forebears encountered, family and social considerations are now greater. With leisure time being more limited any short cut to getting the model ready for flying is welcomed and the ARTF's certainly achieve this aim. Aeromodelling purists may decry the move away from the values of 'traditional' building and finishing of model aeroplanes, but is this fair comment? Some of the first model aeroplanes, sold by toy retailers such as Hamley Bros. of London, almost 100 years ago, were rubber powered 'A' frame pushers and they were RTF. Dick Pavely, a noted aeromodeller for many years sold his designs complete, with hand carved propeller fitted and the Warneford and Skisail models, constructed from spruce and bamboo and covered with silk were also in the completed state. Fast forward to the 30's and the famous name of FROG (Flies right off ground) was behind a whole series of ready to fly models, the most famous being the 'Interceptor'. These models complete with a box which doubled as a support while winding the rubber motor via a geared crank, included rubber lubricant and oil, production

Helicopters were the first model aircraft to be justly called 'Almost ready to Fly', they provided a bolt together assembly rather than a cut and glue construction of conventional fixed wing aeroplane kits.

reached a staggering 1,000 models per day - and the models flew well. Ironically, it is the vintage enthusiasts, the so called purists, who hold these early ARTF's in such high esteem!

International Model Aircraft, manufacturers of the FROG model aircraft, continued with small ready to fly models and although they never produced large free flight or radio ARTF kits they sowed the seeds for this development by introducing moulded balsawood/paper/resin, injection and vacformed mouldings, pressed metal components and even a complete metal structure kit. ARTF models were here to stay.

Progress of ARTF radio control model aircraft was fairly slow, except in one particular area, that of R/C helicopters. From the beginning the helicopter kits were highly prefabricated and constituted a bolt together structure, in comparison to the fixed wing models which tended to be of the glue together style. This prefabrication advanced to a stage where the factory fitted parts increased until they reached the stage today where the helicopter is taken out of the box, fuelled or charged and is ready to fly, some are pre-flown before they leave the factory.

With fixed wing models it was the GRP moulded fuselages and veneered foam wings that came first and I admit to designing a one piece moulded foam wing, manufactured by Micro Mold, in 1970. But these were elements in a package, there was still plenty of building, covering and painting to do before the model could be flown.

It was in the middle 1990's that ARTF model kits, as we know them now, became more widely available with companies such as Thunder Tiger, Kyosho and Robbe introducing them. They were not quite as Ready-to-Fly as some of the modern generation of kits, you certainly had to fit all the control horns, linkages, servo trays, engine mounts etc., but they represented a big advance, in terms of assembly time, compared with the traditional kits. From trainers and sailplanes, plus

Wherever possible obtain the services of an experienced instructor.

a few unconventional designs such as sailwings, the range of types developed to encompass the enormous number of models now on the market. Even more amazing is the fact that the Far Eastern countries, now the major suppliers of the ARTF kits, were never previously recognised as being foremost in the design of model aircraft. Japan was known at one time for being good copiers of

Scale models of full-size aerobatic aircraft are highly popular - but not for the beginner.

Expert instruction is particularly important if you are learning to fly a helicopter.

toy products, but those days have long gone and now China is one of the principal manufacturers of R/C models. Some of the designs are highly innovative and the manufacturers do not rely on Western designers, these are very much home produced and it is a tribute to their invention and industry that so many excellent models come from this source. How do they do it? I understand that only 1% of the Chinese population presently attend University, but that still equates to around one million students and if only a small percentage of these clever and industrious graduates put their skills to designing R/C model aircraft, it still represents a formidable pool of brains and potential.

If you are a newcomer to the hobby and have yet to make any purchases, may I suggest that you read at least chapters 2, 3 and 7 of this book before parting with any hard earned cash, it should help you to avoid making expensive mistakes. Information in the remainder of the book is also important, but can be digested at your leisure, possibly while you are waiting for suitable weather conditions for that all important first flight. You will find some duplication of advice in the chapters, particularly where certain actions are critical, but also to avoid having to constantly move from chapter to chapter.

I hope that you enjoy reading the book and that it is of practical assistance, if it helps to get you safely into the air - and back onto the ground, it will have been worthwhile.

Chapter 2

No Limits to Style or Size

From tiny electric powered foam structure 'toy' models to gas turbine jet powered airframes, all types of model aircraft are now available in ARTF or Ready to Fly (RTF) form. In common with most things in life, you tend to get what you pay for. In other words, if you buy a ready to fly model complete with transmitter, batteries, charger and the model for less than £30, you shouldn't expect to have purchased a sophisticated model capable of serious flying. These small fun models are just that, for fun and should be treated as toys rather than serious flying models. That is not to say that they are not capable, in the right conditions of controlled flight, but there are serious limitations. Some suffer from the manufacturers desire to give maximum value for money by adding as many gimmicks as possible; it might be more effective if they concentrated on the simple values of good flight and control.

Throughout this book there will be reviews of individual kits relevant to the types being discussed in the chapter. It may be, because of the vast numbers of new models coming onto the market, that some specific models are no longer in production, although some of the proven and classic designs are likely to be with us for many years. Even those no longer available will represent a generic type and the general comments will also be applicable to similar models on sale.

Before taking a look at the wider variety of ARTF models a few explanations of the more common abbreviations we use is required; there is a

Although gas turbine powered models of jet prototypes are the most exciting and authentic; they are also the most expensive and demanding of the pilot. A low cost, but effective alternative is an electric powered model with a rear pusher propeller.

glossary of terms and abbreviations at the rear of the book, but some of the more common ones are:-

EP	Electric Power
IC	Internal Combustion engine
R/C	Radio Control
GRP	Glass Reinforced Plastic - for moulding
3D	Three dimensional flying model
CNC	Computer controlled cutting
CAD	Computer Aided design
Rx	Receiver
ESC	Electronic Speed Controller
BEC	Battery Eliminator Circuit
Li-Po	Lithium Polymer battery
NiMh	Nickel Metal Hydride battery
CG	Centre of Gravity (balance point)

Not only has the variety and qualities of the ARTF models increased, but so has the standards of packaging. Brightly coloured boxes with annotations assuring you that you are purchasing the best, the most incredible, the most versatile model imaginable - which will fly right out of your hand - may seduce the unwary into buying. Before you take that irrevocable step do stop and ask yourself a few common sense questions. Do I really need this particular model at this stage? Is the product good value for now and for later? Is the model well constructed? Will the model live up to the promises made on the box artwork? If you do have any doubts ask the proprietor of the hobby shop, this is the advantage of buying from a retailer with expert knowledge and it will save you money in the long run. Try to make a 'Wish List' of the products you require, or think you require, before going to make your purchases, it will help to prevent you buying something on a whim - and regretting it afterwards.

What is the definition of ARTF?

Almost Ready to Fly is a very general term and in practical terms it may refer to less than an hour's work to prepare the model for flight, or it could involve two or three, or even more days effort before you can make that maiden flight. The same

Right: So called pod and boom models make a good introduction to R/C flying, the larger versions are the most practical. Below: For many enthusiasts a model aeroplane has to look like the full-size aeroplane. Ideally you will opt for a non-scale model for your first attempts but if you must go for scale or semi-scale types choose a high wing prototype, such as the Piper Cub.

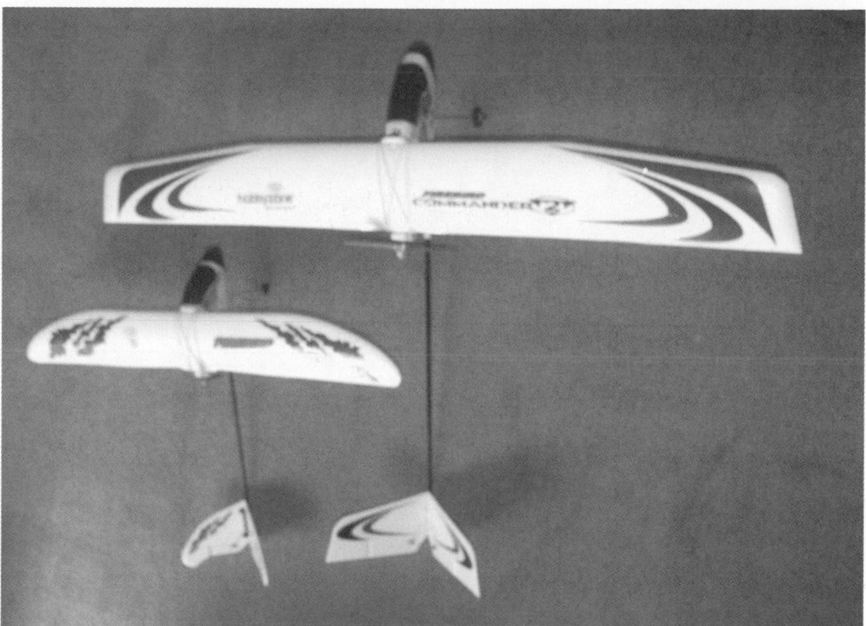

is true of RTF - Ready to Fly models, don't assume that it is automatically 'out of the box and into the air'. In general it is true to say that the assembly of the model and preparing it for flight will take longer than you anticipate, this is especially true when the instructions are less than explicit, or even contain incorrect information. Try not to give yourself a deadline which may be difficult to achieve, assembly should be a pleasurable and exciting phase, not one to be rushed through just to get the model airborne. Also, rushing will probably lead to making errors and jeopardise the chances of successful flight.

Not too small

I mentioned earlier the toy end of the market, with mini-models capable of flight, but not fully

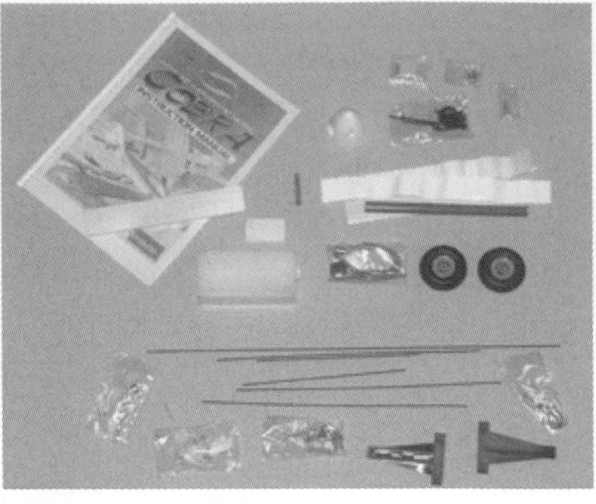

Shoulder and mid-wing models make good advanced trainers and have a good aerobatic performance. Built up balsa and light ply structures are ready covered and decorated and a full complement of accessories are normally included; making the package cost effective.

controlled flight. The next step up from these low cost offerings are two channel conventional designs, often of the pod and boom pusher propeller configuration with a 'V' tail. The "V" tail gives directional control via the elevons (moving control surfaces) on the tail and climb and descent through increasing or decreasing the power to the electric motor. These are fully complete systems, probably on 27mHz frequencies and for an additional outlay it is possible to have selectable control rates, giving you greater control authority when you become a more experienced pilot. The main limitation with a two-channel system is in relation to the ascending and descending through power setting on the electric motor. This will certainly produce a climb or descent but, in a wind, may also result in the model being blown backward, with no penetration into wind. With a three channel model, including elevator control, the versatility is increased and allows the model to be flown in light to moderate winds, depending on the size and wing loading of the model. For training models it is also possible to include what is known as anti-crash technology, in the form of

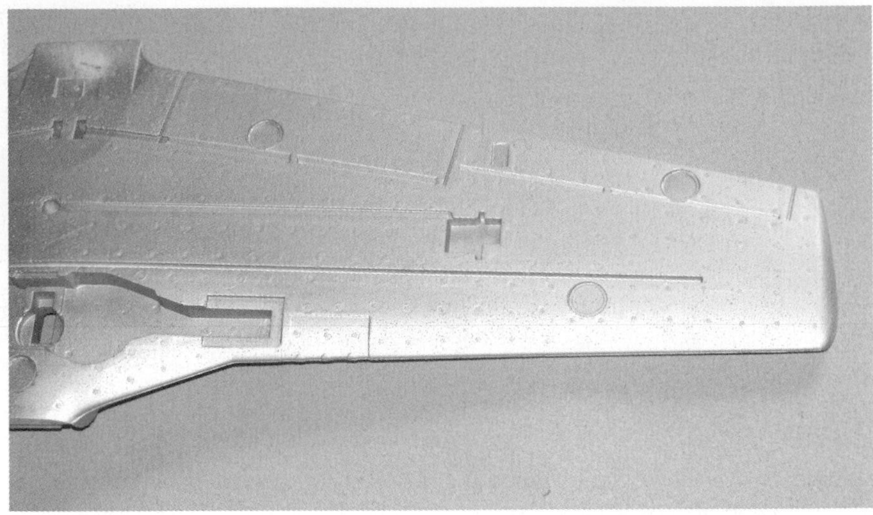

Numerous constructional materials and methods are used in ARTF models, for smaller models (the P-51 Mustang wing is less than a metre span) injection moulded foam gives good results and scale details can be incorporated. See the finished article illustrated overleaf.

an electronic gyro, to prevent over controlling the model and holding-on a transmitter signal until the model assumes a dangerous attitude and would, without intervention, crash. The gyro recognises the extreme attitude and automatically corrects the model irrespective of the control being applied by the pilot. For instance, the pilot may be applying full left control by error, thinking that the model is in a right hand turn, while it is actually spiralling to the left. Unfortunately, it may take the electronic system a while to make this corrective action and it is, therefore, not of great assistance when you are flying fairly low - the most dangerous condition. Complete ready to fly systems, at low cost, also feature scale, or semi-scale models designed to appeal to the 'I want it to look like a real aeroplane' brigade. Because of the compromises made to achieve the scale-like appearance, these models may be more difficult to fly than the non-scale conventional designs, or have poorer flight characteristics. If you are a beginner and insist on a scale-like appearance for the model, choose something like a Piper Cub, or a Cessna and don't be seduced by the lure of an NA Mustang or Supermarine Spitfire. The latter subjects may fly very well, but they need an experienced pilot to get them to perform. Nearly all of these small models feature moulded foam airframes, sometimes with 'hard' foam components, or the softer, more generously proportioned expanded foam; decoration may be painted onto the surfaces, or applied as self adhesive decals.

Trainer size

When it comes to the larger electric trainer models there is less choice of fully complete package outfits that include motor/radio/batteries/charger etc., although there are some good examples to be had and may increase in numbers in the future. For serious training models the implication is that there is an intention to continue with the hobby and therefore some of the equipment will be transferred from the initial training model to later examples. A fully kitted out first trainer would have to contain fairly basic radio equipment to be marketed at a competitive price and this equipment may not be of sufficiently high specification for more advanced models. Unless you can visualise being satisfied with flying fairly simple models it could prove to be uneconomic to

Despite its diminutive proportions, the P-51 Mustang, electric powered, has working retracting undercarriage and flaps.

invest in a full package trainer model. If you do, ensure that the radio is on a 35mHz frequency, with a minimum of four channels and the transmitter includes dual rates and ATV (adjustable travel volume for the servos) and the system utilises rechargeable batteries.

Airframes only

When it comes to ARTF, or RTF, airframes only, or perhaps with just an electric motor fitted, the choice becomes vast. Because of their unique flying qualities, helicopters will be considered as a separate species and we will concentrate on the types available for I.C. engines, electric motors and gliders.

Before ARTF models became available, the normal method of obtaining an airframe was to build one, either from a kit, or from scratch i.e. a plan and the raw materials, and to cover the balsawood and plywood framework with a suitable covering material. These methods of traditional building are still employed on some of the ARTF models, with the added advantage of being jig built for greater accuracy than the individual was likely to achieve. Covering materials are likely to be the heat-shrink films, although the heat sensitive fabrics are used in some cases. Traditional construction methods have the advantage of giving greater flexibility of positioning material precisely where it is needed for maximum strength. Hence, wing panels can be reinforced near the centre where added strength is required, or the fuselage can be reinforced at high stress points such as undercarriage locations or engine bulkheads, this is not always possible to accomplish with fully moulded foam structures. Another theoretical advantage is that following structural damage through a crash, the structure can be repaired; this may only be theoretical because a newcomer to model flying may not have any experience of building traditional airframes and knowledge of how to repair them. Hopefully this book may go a little way to correcting this lack of knowledge.

Plastics have, of course, been employed in the manufacture of model aircraft for many years, initially for 'solid', non-flying models, then for some components, such as propellers and wheels and finally where the complete airframe is produced from plastic. Two of the first materials used were GRP and Styrofoam, the former with glass cloth reinforcement, for moulded fuselages and the latter as a core material for wings, the surface being veneered with balsawood, or obechi wood. These materials were quite labour intensive and time consuming therefore not ideal for mass production methods, but they sufficed until more modern methods and materials could be found. Injection moulding has the disadvantage of relatively high costs for the mould tools, but once these have been produced the actual production costs are low. There is one other snag for the designer and that is in the design of the model. It is virtually impossible to produce an accurate prototype of the finished moulded item. Certain assumptions of weight distribution and strengths have to be made, fortunately the designers rarely seem to get it wrong, otherwise you would have a poor flying model, or they would have the expense of remaking the injection moulding tools. There are very many types of plastic now used in model and toy production and new ones are being developed all the time. Some have completely hard surfaces and cores, like the injection moulded plastic 'solid' model kits, some have a hard skin back-filled with a foam plastic, some form a harder skin from the foam material and others remain in the foam state, like Styrofoam, but have greater strengths than this material. What types of plastics are involved, or the methods used is only of importance to us in respect of gluing the materials together, making repairs and painting. Instruction manuals may not specify the precise plastic compound used, but they will probably advise on the adhesives to use, or not to use; if you are ever uncertain of the compatibility of glues or paints carry out a test on some scrap material first. The same advice applies if you have need to repair or reinforce any part of the moulded airframe, there are few more embarrassing sights than watching a moulded foam component being dissolved through using the wrong adhesive. One of the greatest advantages of injection moulding is that every component from the same mould is virtually identical and replacement parts should be a perfect fit and take the place of the original part without any modification being needed. It also means that the weight distribution of the airframe remains the same in each case and this is important for fully-equipped models, providing the motor, batteries, servos etc., are installed in the same positions, the balance point will be identical on all models. As the CG, or balance point, is one of the critical considerations when it comes to the flying, this is highly important. Aeromodelling has benefited from developments in the area of full-size aircraft. Such materials as carbon-fibre and kevlar may not have become available if they had not been used extensively in the military aircraft business, even the aluminium alloys used for our undercarriage legs had their beginnings in the aircraft industry. No doubt other materials and methods will be developed in the future to give us even more efficient, lighter and stronger models.

What's in a name?

An area of undoubted confusion to a newcomer to R/C model aeroplanes are the names given to particular types of models. Some names are self explanatory, a trainer, for instance, is obviously a model intended for learning to fly and an aerobatics design fairly describes a model with a potential to carry out advanced aerobatic manoeuvres, but other terms are less obvious. Here are a few examples.

Powered Glider

Sounds like a contradiction of terms, as a glider is normally unpowered. It refers to a model with

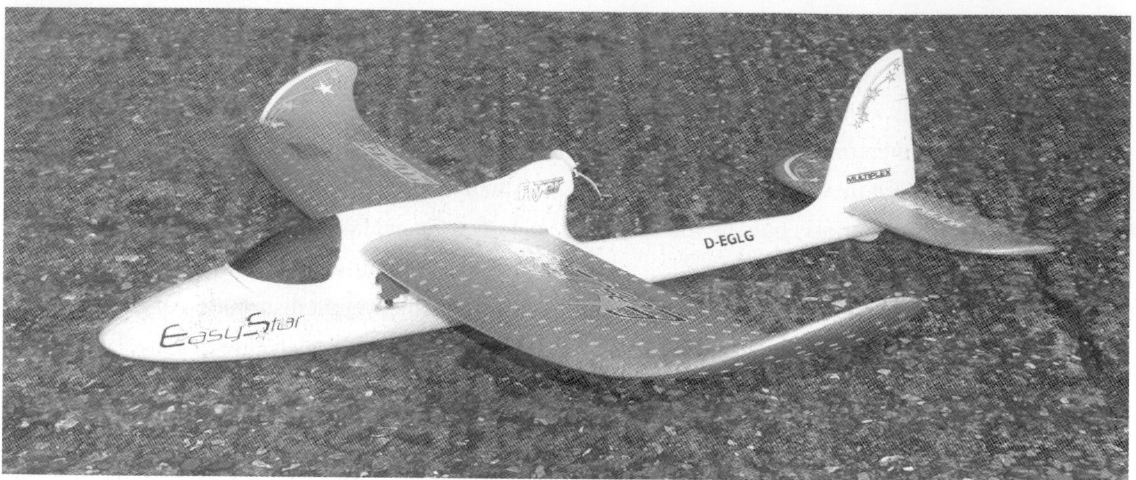

general glider proportions but has a motor, in the nose or above the wing, to take the model to height before the motor is switched off and the model continues in glider mode.

Micro Model

This general term refers to very small R/C models. There are RTF models complete with electric motor/battery/ESC and actuator for controlling the rudder with a total all-up weight, ready to fly, of less than 5 grams! However, the term Micro can refer to anything up to, say, 300mm wing span, the limits tend to get less as miniaturisation of equipment improves.

Indoor

A term which may depend on the size of the indoor room being used for flying, but normally considered to be a sports hall of reasonable dimensions. Highly manoeuvrable designs are

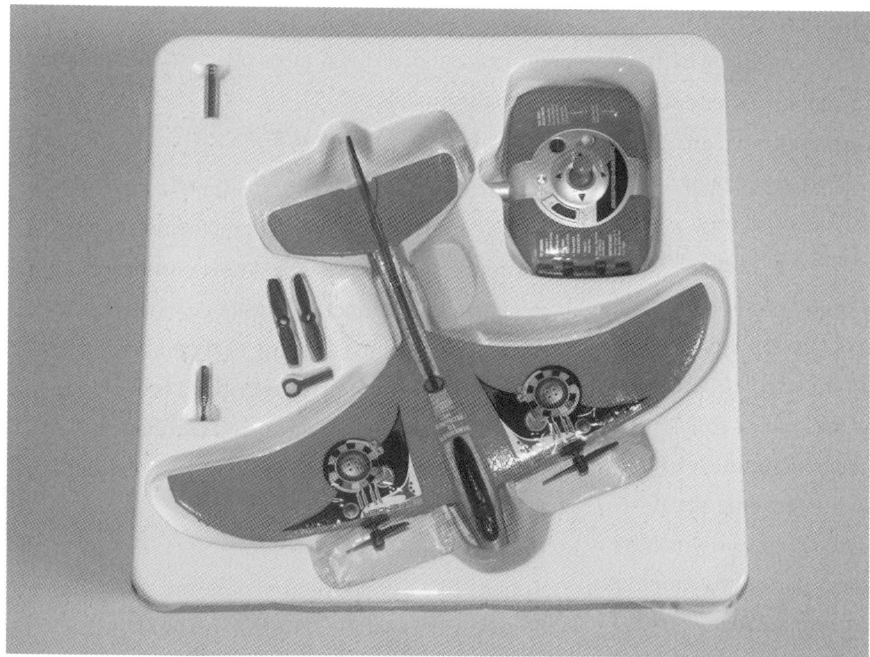

The powered glider layout of the 'Easy Star', above, provides a good starting point, the kit features moulded foam airframe components.
Small, toy electric R/C aeroplanes do fly, but you need ideal weather conditions and a little experienced help, unless you have some flying skills.

particularly suited to indoor flying, provided that you have the skills to be in command of the model all the time. For commencing indoor R/C flying, which are virtually all electric powered, you should choose a simple, non-scale, lightweight model - and this only after you are competent at flying R/C models outdoors. Indoor types can be flown outdoors, but only in totally calm wind conditions such as balmy, summer evenings; this gives the advantage of being able to test and trim the model before committing it to the hazards of walls and the ceiling of an indoor hall.

Park-Flyer

An American term which gives the wrong connotations e.g. a model which can be flown in a public park. Many public park areas in the UK are covered by bye-laws which forbid the flying of all, or certain types of model aircraft. Similarly, advice given

Park flyers are often of the 'Shock Flyer' type where the model, constructed from polystyrene sheet, is capable of 3D manoeuvres, but non-aerobatic models also can come within the Park Flyer category.

to fly from parking lots is not to be taken literally.

School-yard Flyer

Another American term implying the same dangers as Park-Flyer, fine if you can get permission to fly from a school playing area, but otherwise take the terms as meaning suitable for flying from smallish areas.

3D Models

These are capable of performing more than the usual competition aerobatic manoeuvres and can 'prop-hang' i.e. held vertically and also carry out torque turns in that attitude. Lightweight and high power engines or motors are an essential of 3D models which may vary in size from indoor examples to half scale replicas of full-size aerobatic aircraft - which are unable to perform the more extreme aerobatic 3D manoeuvres executed by the models.

The model above is specifically designed for 3D flying, hence the wing fences, but the 'Stick' design can be configured as a simple aerobatic type or, with the addition of 'flaperons' a good 3D trainer.

Floats can be added to most models, including 3D types; waterplane flying adds another dimension to your flying. Flying boats offer an alternative form of waterplane flying.

Shock Flyers

These also are capable of 3D manoeuvrability but tend to be the smaller, all sheet, Depron (a proprietary EP material) models incorporating high performance electric motors, Li-Po batteries and miniature R/C equipment.

In addition to these specialised designs there are the general sports models, scale - in various degrees of accuracy of replication - waterplanes, both float equipped or flying boat, pylon racing designs, combat (for aerial warfare) and vintage types. Power for these RTF and ARTF kits comes in three varieties, electric, internal combustion and gas turbine, the latter 'jet' engines being used mostly in scale models of full-size jet aircraft . These are at the higher cost end of the market and should not be considered, from safety grounds, until you are totally competent and thoroughly experienced with advanced forms of IC powered models, including fast flying scale models.

The term IC engine generally refers to Glow Plug (or Glo Plug) engines, either two or four-stroke types and including multi-cylinder types. There are also a few makes of diesel engines, but these tend to be used only by aficionados of this type of engine, they do tend to be smellier and dirtier than Glo engines, but they also offer greater tractability and will swing large propellers at modest speeds. The kits of the ARTF models will specify engines suitable for powering them, some have IC and electric as alternatives. In addition to purchasing the Glo engine it will be necessary to buy the fuel, propellers and a field box containing a 12 volt battery, power panel, fuel pump and plug energising lead, plus a starter. It is possible to start a Glo motor by hand, dispensing with the 12 volt starter, but this is an acquired skill and modern engines tend to be tight until the first few runs are completed, making it difficult for the beginner to start initially.

EP models and their ancillary equipment are dealt with in Chapter 5.

The ultimate for many R/C flyers and would be flyers, is a fully working scale jet model, powered by a gas turbine engine, operating undercarriage, flaps and possibly, navigation lights.

Helicopters

As previously stated, helicopters are virtually a subject on their own and there are other publications dealing with this form of flying. However, the newcomer to R/C flying will want to know how a helicopter is operated and what is available for them to buy, assemble and fly. With regard to the method of controlling the flight of a helicopter, I can do no better than to repeat the words to be found in the Instruction Manual for the Hoverfly Pro helicopter trainer produced by Snelflight, the subject of a separate review.

"*Conventional helicopters generate lift by means of the rapidly moving rotor blades. A helicopter can have any number of blades from two upwards, which collectively form the* ***rotor****. The blades are shaped as aerofoils, and give the machine its name; 'helico', meaning rotary, and 'pter', meaning wing. The blades are set at an angle to the horizontal, so that they create upward thrust as they turn, like a giant propeller. The angle of inclination of the blades is referred to as their* ***pitch****, and can be changed by the pilot using the helicopter's flight controls. Overall lift is controlled by changing the pitch of all the blades simultaneously. This is referred to as* ***collective control****, and allows the pilot to cause the helicopter to climb or descend. To maintain a steady altitude, the pilot must set the blades so that the lift they provide exactly matches the helicopter's weight.*

Directional control is achieved by varying the pitch of each blade as it travels around its circular path, so that more lift is provided on one half of the rotor disc than on the other. This is referred to as ***cyclic control****, and allows the pilot to tilt the aircraft in any desired direction. For example, in order to make the helicopter's nose drop (as if to dive), the pitch of each blade is reduced as it enters the front semicircle, and increased as it enters the rear semicircle. Less lift*

Before you think of buying 'Spitfire' or Concorde models you must first learn to fly trainer models and the best way of learning is to have some expert tuition, using the 'buddy box' system of control where the transmitters are interlinked

*is then generated at the front than at the rear, causing an imbalance that tilts the whole aircraft. This in turn causes the helicopter to move forward, because the inclined rotor now provides some thrust in this direction, rather than pulling straight upwards as it did when it was spinning horizontally. This is how a helicopter achieves forward flight. The controls of a helicopter allow the pilot to tilt the aircraft from side to side (**roll**) as well as from front to back (**pitch**, not to be confused with blade pitch!), and any combination of the two, giving total freedom of movement. Constant adjustment of these controls allows the pilot to keep the machine exactly horizontal, and thus to hover.*

*The mechanism that achieves these control functions is complex, and involves numerous mechanical linkages and push-rods, as well as a special tiltable bearing called the **swash-plate**. In the case of models, servos are needed in addition, to provide physical actuation of the control mechanisms.*

It is important to realise that a helicopter does not hover or fly by itself, but requires continuous fine adjustment of the controls to maintain stability in the air. The skill required to do this has to be learned, and is fundamental to helicopter flying. However, a helicopter derives a good deal of stability from the rotating blades, which act as a large gyroscope. This slows down its rate of response to a speed at which a human pilot can control it, with practice!

*The rotor of a helicopter is generally driven by an engine mounted in the fuselage, by means of a large central drive shaft. In order to make the rotor turn, the engine has to push against its mountings. This means that the engine is actually trying to turn the helicopter fuselage just as hard as it is turning the rotor itself. This unwanted turning force is referred to as a **torque reaction**.*

*In order to prevent the fuselage from spinning, a helicopter is fitted with a **tail rotor**, which is simply a propeller mounted sideways on the tip of the tail, which pulls against the turning force from the engine. The tail rotor's thrust can be changed, by altering the pitch of its blades. This allows the pilot to steer the aircraft in the horizontal plane, an action referred to as **yaw**.*

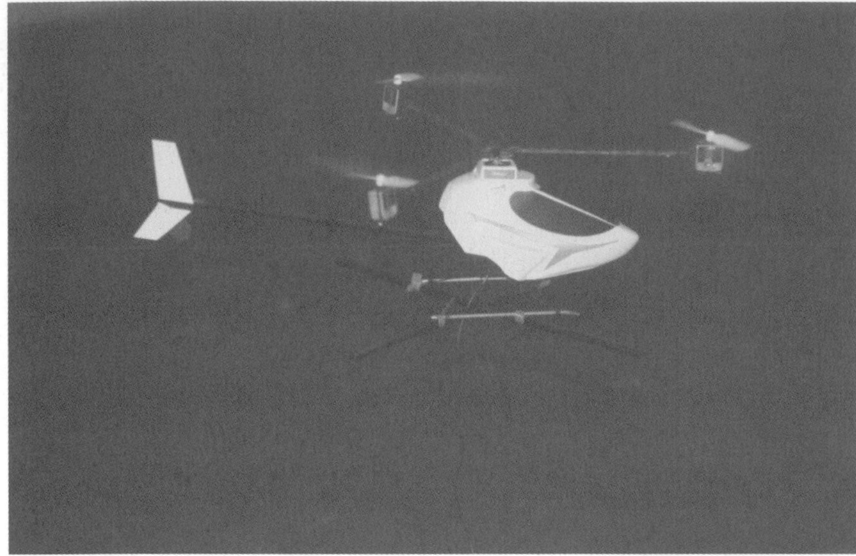

Helicopters are almost a subject apart, but an excellent way of learning to fly is by flying small indoor heli models, or a training helicopter, such as the 'Hoverfly Pro', (left). Easier to fly, but more limited in control movements, are the twin rotor electric models (below), available at very modest prices.

The control has the same effect as a ship's rudder, except that it works even while the aircraft is stationary in the air.

Learning to use this control to keep the helicopter pointing in a desired direction is a further challenge for a new pilot. It has to be done whilst at the same time keeping control over the other axes of movement, which requires great concentration for a beginner. Because the pilot of a model is not actually inside the aircraft, confusion tends to result when the machine is pointing towards him/her. The aircraft's left hand side becomes the pilot's right hand side, and vice versa. The pilot has to be constantly aware of this in order to remain in control".

In common with fixed wing model aeroplanes, helicopters can be powered by all three power sources, can be scale or freelance design, can be for indoors or outdoors and include aerobatic and 3D types. They also come in varying stages of readiness for flight ranging from those requiring a few days assembly and preparation time to those which have been test flown at the factory before they are sold; the costs also vary considerably

At the top end of competitions you will see very large ARTF aerobatic models and helicopters capable of executing extreme 3D manoeuvres

depending on the size and complexity. There is no doubt that helicopter flying, being more demanding than flying fixed wing models, will benefit from the would-be pilot practising with a training aid, such as the Snelflight Hoverfly Pro, or a Model Flight Simulator, the latter will obviously have to be operated in conjunction with a compatible computer. There is also no doubt that the availability of indoor EP helicopters, with specifications and control systems the equivalent to the more expensive I.C. outdoor heli's have encouraged many more enthusiasts, normally fixed wing model only flyers, to try their hand at helicopter flying. They can be flown in reasonably confined areas, school halls etc., and are very reasonably priced, a complete system can cost less than £200 and they can be flown

There may come a time when you want to emulate these experts, by which time you will have no need for thei book!

Although the author has designed hundreds of R/C model aeroplanes, over a 50 year period, he also enjoys assembling and flying ARTF models and has a high regard for many of the designs.

outdoors in calm conditions.

For an even easier introduction to rotary wing model flying, the twin rotor designs where one rotor is positioned above the other, on the same vertical shaft, offers a more rapid way of becoming a proficient pilot. Although these machines have more limitations in respect of extreme flight manoeuvres, they are certainly capable of giving satisfying flying and plenty of fun at very competitive costs. They should not be discounted as 'only toys', they can give a good indication of whether or not rotary wing flying is for you, at a price that won't break the bank and you can then, if you wish, transfer to more sophisticated helicopters.

Chapter 3
In the Beginning

A mixture of the old and the new, a vintage style design produced in an ARTF form; it has electric power and performance to suit a beginner.

Whereas learning to drive a radio controlled car or boat can be comparatively easy and painless, the same is not truc with a model aeroplane. With a car you only have to reduce power and it will stop, the worst that can happen is that you might hit an object and it is unlikely that, through a control error, you will sink a boat. With an aeroplane there is no stopping in mid-air and deciding what action to take, slow it up too much and it will fall, uncontrolled, to the ground. In a sense, you have to be a competent pilot from the moment the aeroplane leaves your, or a colleague's hand; once airborne it must be controlled and eventually landed. Irrespective of what the model kit manufacturers may intimate, this is not the easiest of undertakings, even with the most 'trainer friendly' designs, the beginner will need all the help he can get to achieve a level of skill where he can fly solo with reliability and safety. Incidentally, I am not intentionally being sexist when referring to 'he', the hobby is just as suitable for the ladies, it is just a shame that more do not participate in building and flying radio control model aircraft.

Notice, at the end of the last paragraph, I refer to aircraft, because the term aeroplane is technically 'a powered heavier-than-air flying vehicle with fixed wings' and we are also considering gliders and helicopters, the latter being almost a separate branch of the hobby.

Putting helicopters to one side for the moment, the beginner has two choices of fixed wing models to consider: powered or gliders. Although gliders, or sailplanes as they are sometimes called, are a reasonable alternative for learning to fly R/C models you really need a good slope soaring site near to you, where you can rely on the upcurrents of air to sustain flight. Tracing the locations of slope soaring sites is best achieved by contacting the BMFA (see Chapter 10) or visiting specialist

Not precisely a powered glider, but a semi-scale model of a full-size type with excellent glide performance. Typical of the three channel, complete with radio models widely available.

web-sites. Not pure sailplanes, but a compromise between power and glider, are the powered gliders where you have an airframe design similar to a glider and with an electric motor in the nose, usually with a folding propeller. This allows you to climb to height, where the power is switched off and the model continues in a gliding mode until the motor is switched on again to recover height. These models are elegant and efficient, do not feature undercarriages or, frequently, aileron control. Limitations include flying only when wind conditions are right, when you are training, and because of the efficient glide where you lose height slowly, the need for a flying site where the landing approaches, are free from obstructions. Powered gliders are seldom suitable for progressing onto the next phase of training, where you will be performing aerobatics, but they can be an economic way of taking those first steps into R/C flying. Most commonly the EP gliders have moulded plastic or glass-fibre fuselages and built-up, open structure flying surfaces, ready covered, with the electric motor also supplied. With the high degree of prefabrication and fitting of motor and control linkages it is only a matter of fitting the servos, receiver and battery and the model is ready for flight; the longest delay may be in charging the battery - and waiting for suitable weather conditions. If you decide to take this approach to R/C flying look for designs with wing spans of around 70ins (1800mm) to 87ins (2200mm) these will give the stability and visibility necessary for a trainer. I would not recommend purchasing a kit complete with radio equipment in this case as it would probably be installed with a 27mHz; three channel transmitter (single stick with a motor control switch or slider control) and you will want to progress onto more sophisticated control equipment before long. Fortunately there are plenty of good electric glider designs available

Before purchasing a kit check what the contents consist of and the quality, if in doubt refer to the magazine reviews. The Graduate (reviewed later) is a good example of a well-produced ARTF kit.

which are suitable for installing your own radio equipment (see Chapter 4).

Conventional Training Models

What is a conventional trainer? We are normally considering a model that represents, to a greater or lesser degree, a modern full-size light aircraft, such as one of the Cessnas or Pipers. When I was designing and manufacturing model aircraft kits I made a classic mistake, I assumed that because a trainer with a shoulder wing location (no cabin) would fly as well as, and probably better than a cabin style, high wing design, that it would sell well. Wrong! Newcomers to the hobby wanted a model that 'would look like a real aeroplane' and ultimately the customer is right. Hence, R/C trainers tend to follow the pattern of a slab-sided fuselage, with the cabin painted on (or indicated with contrasting film covering) and a high wing location. There are exceptions, often amongst the EP trainers and as we elaborate on the traditional IC powered trainers later, we will first consider the EP trainers.

Quiet and clean

To some extent there are two types of model aircraft enthusiasts: those that appreciate the cleanliness and silence, nearly, of electric power and others that like the challenge of starting and operating IC engines who delight in the sounds and smells and don't mind getting a bit dirty and oily, they may even revel in it (guilty!) As electric flight becoming evermore popular, efficient and cost effective it makes sense for enthusiasts of this form of flying to start with an EP trainer. Look through the advertisements and catalogues and you will not find too many genuine, specific EP trainers. Yes, there are plenty of kits that are described as suitable for training, or fly as easyily as a trainer, but few that are designed as dedicated training models. Why this is so is discussed later, it is a situation that is bound to be rectified rapidly; until then we must look for the best alternatives on the market. There are plenty of smallish, 30 to 40ins (750 to 1000mm) models complete with motor, radio equipment, batteries and charger that profess to be suitable for training, but these are not suitable for serious learning. They are often semi-scale in appearance, attractive and desirable, but you should be looking for something larger for a first R/C model. I have already mentioned the powered sailplanes as a suitable trainer and there are also some 'pod and boom', with a pusher motor, which fill the bill, but opt for those with a wing span in excess of

1000mm. In contrast to the kits that claim to be 'ideal' trainers, the larger pod and boom models may be advertised as sporty and having combat and dropping facilities, but make more suitable trainers due to their size (typically 1200 – 1300mm). Such models have injection moulded airframes and provided that the transmitter includes rate switching of the control movements, are good trainers, the motor is typically in the 540 series, with rechargeable 1700 to 2000mAh batteries. These designs will cope with moderate wind conditions and once you have mastered the controls, can be aerobatted at the higher rate settings and feature very rapid assembly. Supplied complete with radio equipment, the airborne radio is not readily accessible, the fuselage has to be broken open to retrieve the components. Flight is a mixture of powering up to height and then cutting the motor to glide.

Old Time

Slowly does it with the vintage style electric models. These are open frame, film covered, with a light wing loading and stately flight, definitely not for the go-getting youngsters keen to try their hand at aerobatics as soon as possible. The down side of these models is that because of their slow flying characteristics, they are really only suited to those calm, balmy days. True vintage models are rarely found as ARTF kits, it is almost a contradiction of terms. There are a number of 'lookalike', models that have open structures and feature high degrees of stability, the principle differences being that they are now covered in heat shrink film instead of the traditional tissue, silk or nylon and are EP rather than IC powered. Vintage style designs are normally three function controlled. Ailerons are not very effective on models with generous wing dihedral even so, it is normal to fly them using the aileron control stick on the transmitter for operating the rudder. When you move on to a four function model you will have to learn to control the rudder with the left hand stick on the transmitter and aileron from the right hand stick.

With the incredible advances in electric motors and even more so with rechargeable batteries, there is no shortage of power, or flight duration with EP models. Flight times in excess of 20 minutes are the norm and if you are at the learning stage 10 minutes of concentration will be about your limit. For a newcomer to R/C flying and electric flight, the problems arise because of the choice of equipment available, not only from the motors, brushed versus brushless, outrunners, electric speed controllers (ESC) batteries, NiCad, NiMH and Li-Po's (and more variations on the way) charger types and meters, gear boxes and propellers, it is a potential minefield. How do you make sense of this bewildering and ever increasing array of EP goodies? Initially you don't, you go for a recommended package of motor/propeller/ESC/battery combination for a specific model. If you then decide to stick with electrics you will progress onto more advanced models and power systems, read the specialist articles in magazines and learn from fellow enthusiasts. Don't aim too high for your first EP purchases, make haste slowly and you will find an electrical paradise waiting for you in the future. EP will be discussed in greater detail in Chapter 5.

Reading the glossy advertisements in model magazines may give a false impression with regard to the general availability of trainer models kits. Perusing an 8 page advertisement for R/C kits, motors, radio equipment and accessories there were only two dedicated trainer models included

Some ARTF models, such as the Multiplex Magister, can be electric or IC powered as shown with the Hobbyzone 'Commander' (below). Introduction level kits will often include the 'complete works', including transmitter and charger for the airborne battery.

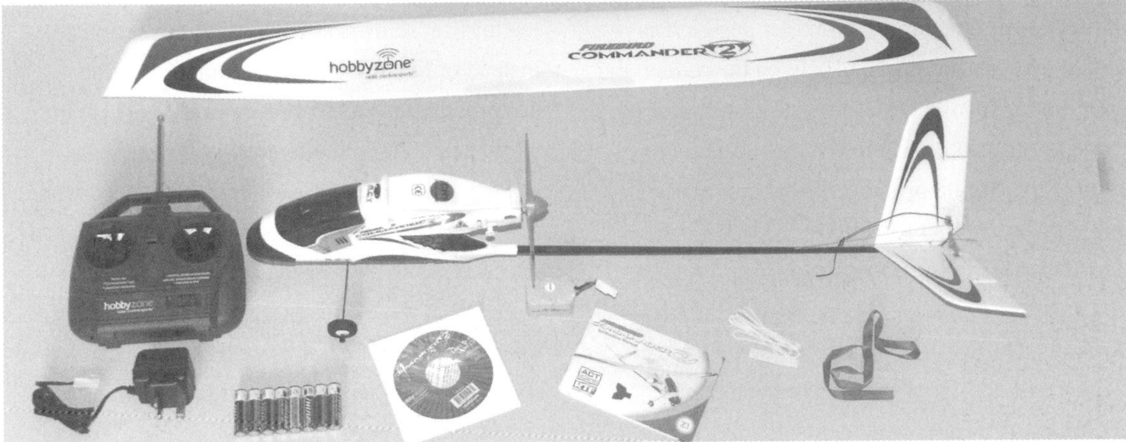

in the hundreds of items mentioned; this is not because the trainer is not important, it is because it doesn't make such exciting copy as other types. Also, new real trainers do not come out from recognised manufacturers very frequently. There is no point in being different just for difference sake and once a training model is well established it will stay in the market for a long time; it is the more exotic model types that have to be constantly reinvented.

Because the '40' size trainer (for engines of approximately 0.40cu.in. capacity) has been, and is at present the most popular way of learning to fly R/C model aircraft I am devoting quite a few pages and reviews to this type. With a changing market moving more towards EP this situation may alter, and after the detailed section on the IC trainer, I will devote more words to electric power and the models associated with this motive force. Many of the general comments made in the section dealing with the traditional IC trainer will be equally applicable to EP trainer models, so please don't assume that, if you are taking the EP path, that there is nothing of value in that chapter.

The traditional ARTF Trainer

Since the inception of ARTF radio control model aircraft, the basic trainer powered by an IC engine has been the highest volume seller of all the kits. The reason for this is not difficult to see, it is the introduction to R/C model flying and we all have to learn to fly before we can go on to other forms of models. Although there are a few variations, the basic trainer tends to be a high, or shoulder wing design with a parallel chord wing of modest dihedral; the fuselage is long, with good moment arms to the engine and tail surfaces, the latter having generous proportions. A tricycle undercarriage is fitted, the nose-wheel is normally steerable and glo engine around the '40' size (0.40cu.in) provides the power. Wing spans of 60ins (1550mm) are the norm, although smaller models, with engines down to '25' size are available. The larger models are controlled by four channel radio, operating the ailerons, elevator, rudder and engine throttle. Smaller designs may omit the aileron control and rely on the rudder and increased wing dihedral, for turning and stability. Contents of the kits, in the UK, are unlikely to include the engine or radio equipment, although this may be the way forward in the future where the newcomer to the hobby is looking for as much assistance in preparing the model for flight as possible. The average ARTF traditional style trainer will consist of the ready covered and decorated airframe components, the fuselage, wing half panels, tail surfaces, these may have the control surfaces ready hinged or they may just have the surfaces slotted ready for you to glue the hinges in position. Control surface horns may also be pre-fitted, in many of the kits you will have to locate the horns and screw them in position. You would expect to find the undercarriage and wheels supplied, (including collets to retain the wheels), a fuel tank – (but not always the fuel tubing lines), engine mount, (possibly pre-fitted), wing joiner, pushrods and guide tubes, clevises, retainers, nuts and bolts. Adhesives are not included, but a well illustrated and clearly written instruction book or manual is an essential. An engine spinner may be included, but not always and foam plastic packing for the radio equipment. Providing that transport or storage is not a problem, I would certainly suggest opting for the 60ins wing span, or thereabouts, model using a '40' sized glo engine. This is large enough to see in the air easily, will cope with moderately windy conditions, say up to 10mph, and has a stability in the air lacking in some of the smaller types.

Assuming that you are going to have some assistance in learning to fly the model, particularly with the help of a 'buddy box' learning system, it is worthwhile considering the purchase of a model featuring a 'semi-symmetrical' wing section i.e. instead of having a wing section with a flat bottom, this surface is also cambered. This will allow you to fly in moderate winds, it will also allow you to progress and learn basic aerobatics. Conversely, if you only expect to have a minimum of experienced help when you are learning to fly, it would be advisable to opt for the lower powered, three channel models as these have a greater degree of positive stability and self-righting qualities and only having to cope with three controls, elevator/ rudder/throttle, may be less daunting. You will, however, be more limited in the weather conditions when you can safely fly your trainer.

At present, and things change rapidly, there are no electric powered direct equivalents to the IC powered basic trainers. This is slightly odd as the new generation of electric motors and lithium LiPo batteries can equal the IC engines in power to weight ratios. You are more likely to find electric powered 'trainers' that are smaller moulded foam semi-scale designs, or powered glider types. The latter should not be discounted as a way into learning to fly, but they will be less suited to windier conditions.

Look and ask

Having decided on the parameters for our powered basic trainer model we can start to look for suitable models. Probably the first thing you will notice is that there is quite a price range for what, ostensibly, are all the same type of product. The box lids will be equally colourful and promising a model that is an ideal trainer, the contents will be similar, but the retail prices will vary considerably. So how do you decide which kit to purchase and will give both the best value and the possibility of a good service life? As a beginner you will only have a vague idea of what to look for in a kit and you could be tempted to buy the wrong product. The answer is to take an experienced modeller along with you to the model shop, or be advised by the model shop proprietor - providing that it is a genuine model retailer and not just a toy shop. A genuine salesman will be an experienced flyer and will know where the local club is and be a member of the club. If you are purchasing by mail order and do not have a direct contact with an experienced modeller, subscribe to a specialist R/C model magazine and read the kit reviews. Even if it doesn't include a specific trainer review it will give a good idea of the qualities of particular manufacturers.

You will notice in the magazine advertisements for 'package deals' where you can purchase the kit and engine and possibly the radio equipment too, for an advantageous price. These are only bargains if the individual products are items you definitely require and, of course, if the total cost is considerably less than the sum total of the parts. One final warning before you make that decision and part with your cash. There will be lots of tempting, exotic and highly desirable kits on display, some may even claim to be trainers, ignore them and concentrate on the standard trainer. Have patience, learn to fly first and then you can move onto the more way-out and extreme designs.

Pitfalls and precautions

Most of the ARTF kits are well produced and fit for their purpose, but there can be problems with some of the models, not always the cheapest on the market.

Covering

Earlier kits tended to be covered with 'sticky-back' film material and although this looks attractive enough it is not easy to deal with when it sags. The instructions will normally say that if the covering slackens use a covering iron, or heat gun to regain its tautness. From experience I have found that this approach rarely gives the desired results. With models covered with 'proper' heat shrink materials (Ultra Cote, Polycote etc), there are no such problems with tautening slackened covering, just don't be tempted to apply too much heat. All of the models have highly decorative colour schemes, some achieve this by using different coloured films plus decals, others use a multi-coloured printed film. In general the covering standards are way above those we could manage. Why? Simply because the worker in the factory applying the covering is carrying out this task day-in day-out and naturally gets very good at the process.

Airframes

How on earth do they manage to produce the ARTF kits at the low prices they are sold? When you add up the costs of the raw materials, accessories and covering materials you would be hard pressed to build a model from scratch for the same money. The vast majority of the kits are produced in China and although labour costs are low they have to import some of the raw materials. Balsawood remains one of the best raw materials for the construction of the airframe, it is both strong and light, but as far as I am aware, this is not an indigenous material in China - I wouldn't

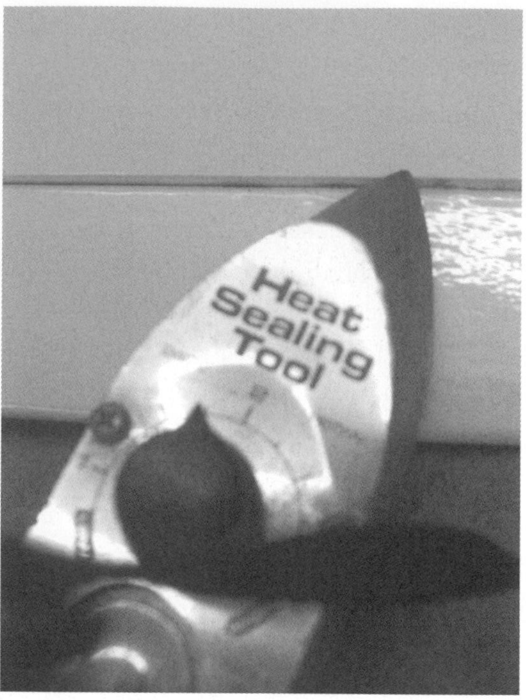

Any slackened covering should be ironed to tauten and openings where film has been cut away should be carefully sealed with an iron. A touch of fuel-proofer will further seal the edges.

take any bets on that situation remaining for long. There are alternative materials to balsawood, Liteply is one of them. Good quality, light balsawood does not come cheap with the result that the lower cost ARTF's may incorporate inferior, heavier balsawood or more plywood in their designs. This does not mean that the structure is liable to failure in the air, it does, however, result in a heavier airframe which, in turn, may affect the flying qualities and if it should crash, or have a heavy landing, is more likely to result in a breakage. In particular, if the tail surfaces are built from heavy wood it may result in the model being tail heavy and the need for some further weight being added to the nose, which will also add to the overall wing loading of the model.

Although it is impossible to inspect the complete airframe of an ARTF model, due to the covering, there are enough cover-free areas to obtain a good impression of the structural integrity of the airframe. The wood components should fit precisely, there should not be too much glue spread over the joints, in other words, the workmanship should be to a good standard. As the airframe components are jig built there should be no misalignment of the structures, no warps (twists) and the fits of the wing and tail surfaces should be accurate. This is a primary reason why you are more likely to have flying success with an ARTF model than with your first attempt at building a model yourself.

In efforts to avoid the variations which are bound to occur in balsa and other woods as they are natural materials, some manufacturers have gone down a different material route. Early ARTF's featured moulded, Plura (a rotationally moulded thermo-plastic), fuselages with veneered foam flying surfaces, all moulded foam models have

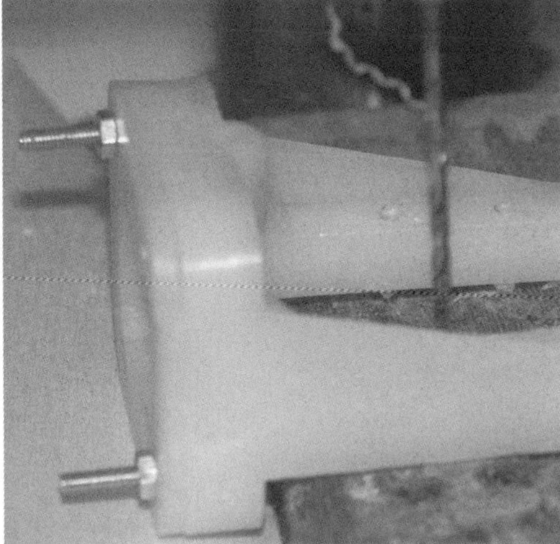

Some engine mounts are supplied with separate mounting lugs to give with adjustment (top left). Position the engine on the mount, measure to give the correct location of the propeller drive, mark the location of the engine bolts, remove the mount from the fuselage and drill the holes for the engine mounting screws.

also been tried, but these are more successful with EP. The most successful of the plastic models are those using injection moulding techniques. Properly designed and using accurate tool making, these models can be very good and they are totally repeatable i.e. a second model will fly almost identically to the previous one. The one downside to these all moulded types is that they tend to have a heavier wing loading than those constructed traditionally, this is partly overcome by using a thick, semi-symmetrical wing section which helps to reduce the stalling speed.

Engine mount

Two types of engine mounts are used in ARTF kits, one of which is the cast metal mount; the engine is secured to the mount by two metal

With the engine firmly mounted, fuel lines attached and cowling securing blocks fitted, the cowling can be marked and cut to fit over the engine. A Dremel Moto-tool, with cutting disc and rotary shaper will make the cowl cutting operation much easier.

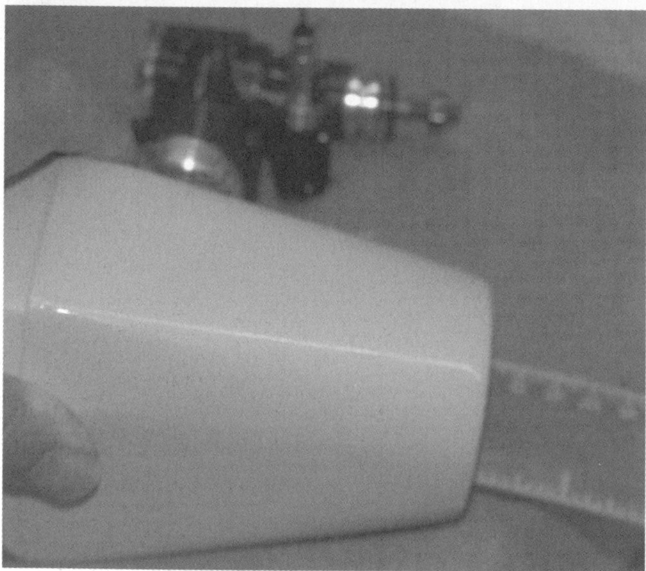

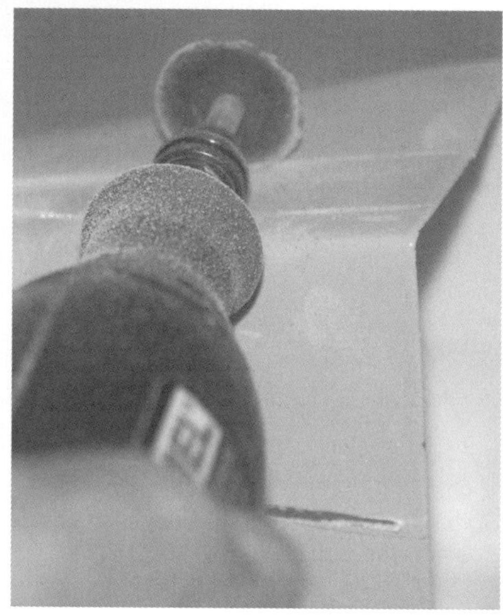

plates, positioned over the engine bearer lugs and held down by nuts and bolts at either end of the plates. This arrangement gives a good latitude on the size of engine to be fitted. Alternatively moulded nylon mounts can be supplied, either in the form of a single piece, or as separate 'T' pieces. In all cases the mounts are bolted to the fuselage front bulkhead, sometimes referred to as a firewall. It is important that the mounts and the engine are securely mounted, a touch of threadlock on the screws will help to prevent them unscrewing, but make it a little more difficult if you have to remove them.

Securing the engine mount to the bulkhead will normally involve fitting screws through the mounts and bulkhead to anchor nuts usually in

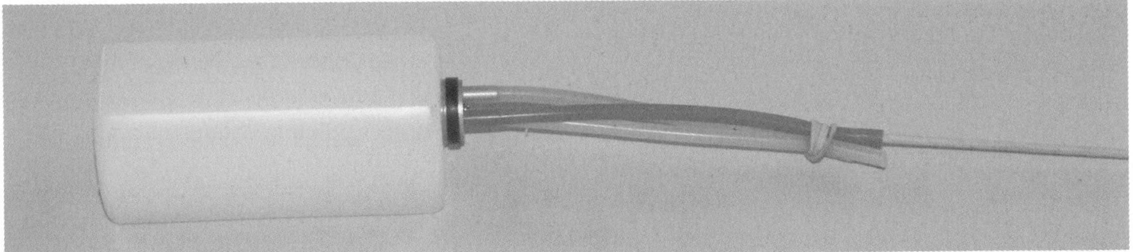

Remove any burrs from the edges of the pipes, you may have to drill out the holes in the plates and stoppers. Use a skewer to hold the fuel lines together when feeding them through the engine bulkhead (above) and apply silicone sealant to fuelproof the area (below).

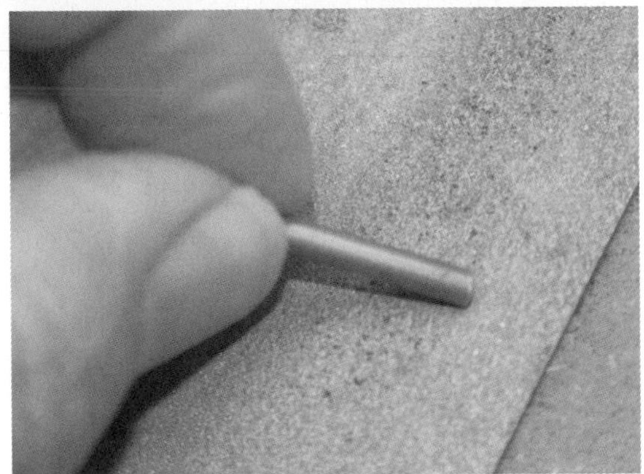

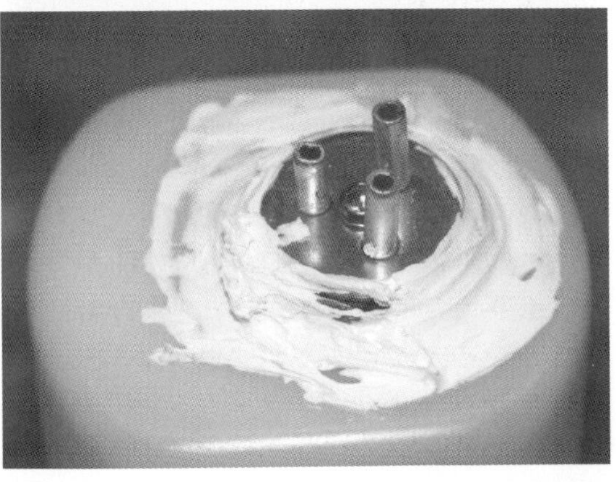

the form of 'T' nuts with spikes that 'bite' into the plywood firewall. Unfortunately these 'T' nuts may not be fully secured and are all too easily pushed out when locating the mount screws, it can then be a very difficult job in relocating the nuts. As a precautionary measure it is prudent to take a large diameter washer, fit the screw carefully into the 'T' nut and tighten the screw to pull the nut securely into the rear of the bulkhead. If you can also apply some epoxy to the perimeter of the nuts, this will further secure the nuts. If you do lose a 'T' nut, or they are not pre-fitted, it may be necessary to cyanoacrylate (cyano or 'super-glue) the nut on the end of a piece of dowel or strip balsawood, in order to locate it in the holes in the bulkhead.

Fuel tanks

Regrettably manufacturers often insist on supplying fuel tanks with only two fuel pipes - one for fuel supply to the engine and one to the engine silencer (muffler) to pressurise the fuel tank and give a more consistent engine run. Where the engine fuel feed nipple is easily accessible this is no great problem, although constant removal and fitting of the tube could cause a split. Where you have a cowled engine it can be a total frustration and in these

To obtain a firm fitting of the wheel collets file a groove at the screw location. Undercarriage bends are radiused; the wood supports must also have the holes radiused to obtain a snug fit.

circumstances the two-pipe tank should be replaced with a three-pipe version, the third pipe acting as a filler that is closed-off with a small stopper once the tank is filled.

Some modellers recommend fitting an inline fuel filter in the fuel feed line to the engine; these two part filters are a possible source of air getting into the system, causing erratic running. Filtering the fuel as it is introduced into the tank is to be preferred. Whether or not the fuel tank is supplied assembled or not, check that the metal tubes projecting at the front of the tank are free from any burrs and fit the fuel tubing while everything is dry, they will stay in position better. You should also check, on a two-pipe tank, internally, to ensure the vents are positioned such that the tank can be filled to capacity and that the weighted clunk is free to move in the tank.

Undercarriages

Again, there are two types of undercarriages supplied with the ARTF trainer, the pressed aluminium alloy main undercarriage, or the bent pianowire legs; the nose leg is invariably a pre-formed pianowire item with a shock absorbing coil. Wheels have moulded plastic hubs and moulded plastic/rubber tyres. For lighter models the tyres may be from moulded foam. Normal wheel retention consists of collets, or collars fitted either side of the pianowire axle. For the alloy or carbon fibre undercarriage separate axles are fitted in the form of bolts and nuts. Where collets are used as retainers locked in place with grub screws, it is essential to grind, or file a flat on the pianowire where the fixing screw locates. This also applies to the steering arm on the nosewheel. A more secure method of holding the wheels in position is to solder washers either side of the wheels, using a piece of metal foil between the washer and the wheel as a heat sink when soldering.

When a first attempt to fit the wheels on the pianowire is made you may find that it is almost impossible to push them into position. It may be that the holes in the wheels are too small, but it is more likely that there are slight burrs on the ends of the wires and these are preventing the wheels being pushed-on. Before you drill out the wheel

Before joining the wing halves ensure that they are an accurate fit, including the dihedral brace (wing joiner). Glue the joiner to one half and then epoxy the other half in position, holding them together with clamps and tape (overleaf)

hubs try filing down the pianowire ends. To make a model more attractive the manufacturers may supply wheel spats, a la full-size light aircraft, if these are included in the kit, throw them away. You will have enough to worry about without having to try not to damage wheel spats during a stressful landing.

Wing joiners

Built-up trainer wings are supplied in left and right hand panels which are then joined by the purchaser. The reason for this is that the finished wing will have some dihedral incorporated (upward angles when viewed from the front) to aid stability and a one piece wing would be difficult to pack - and also result in a very large box. Strength is supplied at the wing joint by dihedral braces, also called wing joiners, which project into the wing panels at their roots. Plywood is often used for this joiner, although they can also take the form of light alloy tubes, or rectangular section alloy reinforced internally with plywood. Where a tube is used it normally relies on the housing in plywood wing ribs for its strength of fitting, plywood and aluminium tube rectangular joiners fit into a housing formed in the wing panel structure. Check the fit of the joiner in the housing, it should not be too tight otherwise, when the adhesive is applied it will be impossible to push it in position. Even if 5 minute epoxy is recommended for this purpose use the 20 minute version. It will give you more time to correctly position the joiner and wings and prevent panic!

Accessories

This is where the manufacturers of ARTF kits are most likely to fail, in the supply of accessories such as control horns, clevises, keepers, adapters, connectors etc. Common faults include clevises, with holes that are too large and are only a push fit on the screw ends of the metal pushrods - a very dangerous situation. Conversely the holes in the clevises may be too small to allow them to be threaded onto the rod without having to use

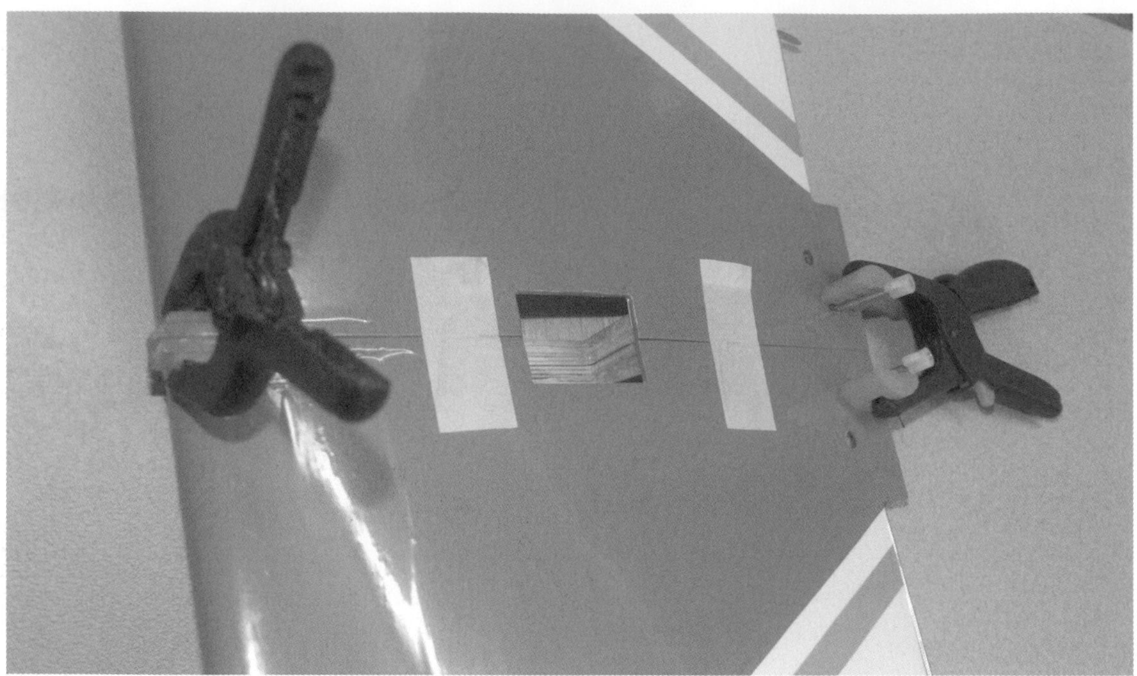

excessive force, which would make it impossible to adjust on the model. Control horns need to be firmly secured to the control surfaces and the screws, or self-tappers may be of the wrong diameter, or length, to achieve this aim. When the same company is supplying the control horns and the clevises, why is it that the clevis pins will not fit into the horns? The same applies to the moulded nylon keepers, which retain the pushrod with a 90 degrees bend where it is fitted to the servo output arm and the wire is too thick for the keeper to be fitted without a Herculean effort. Clevises have a safety feature to prevent them from accidentally coming adrift, this takes the form of a piece of silicone, or similar tubing which is slipped over the jaws of the clevis to prevent them opening. It is pointless supplying tubing with such a small diameter that it cannot be stretched over the clevis. These may be considered as small criticisms but they are highly frustrating, especially when the modeller is keen to get the model finished and to go flying.

Most common arrangement for pushrods, (whether they take the form of a continuous metal rod, a plastic tube inside another plastic tube e.g. 'snake', or a wooden rod with metal rods at each end), is to have an adjustable clevis at one end and a 90 degrees bend and keeper at the other end. It may, however, have adjustment to the pushrod length at the servo in the form of connectors which are fitted to the servo, and are free to rotate and hold the metal pushrod by a small screw. Although I have used these successfully on small models often using nylon rod inner and plastic tube outer pushrods, I would hesitate to use them on larger and heavier trainers. If you are in any doubt about the suitability or strength of the supplied accessories, have a word with a model shop proprietor and purchase some replacements, it will save you money in the long run.

Instructions

It would be marvellous to be able to state that the

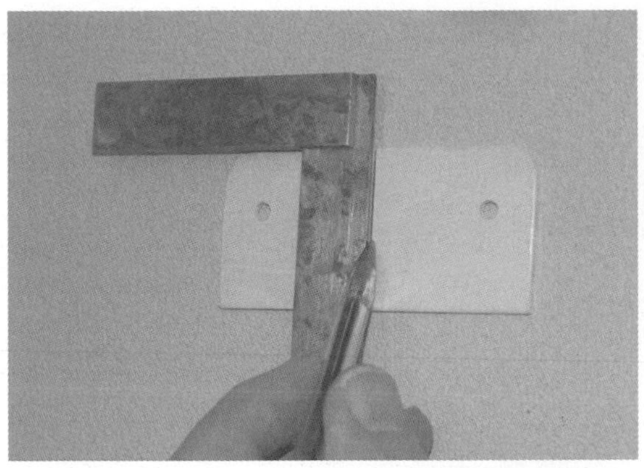

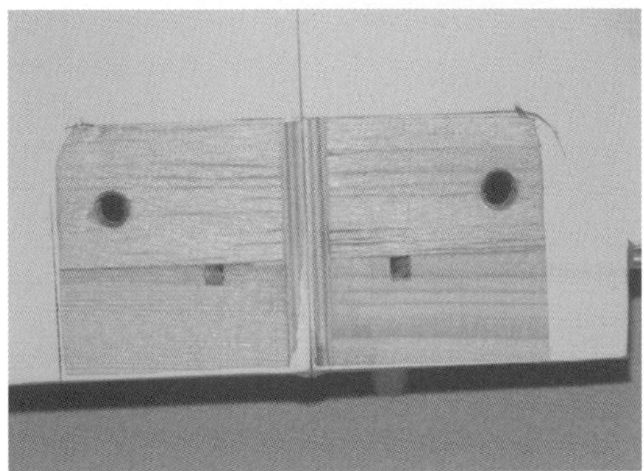

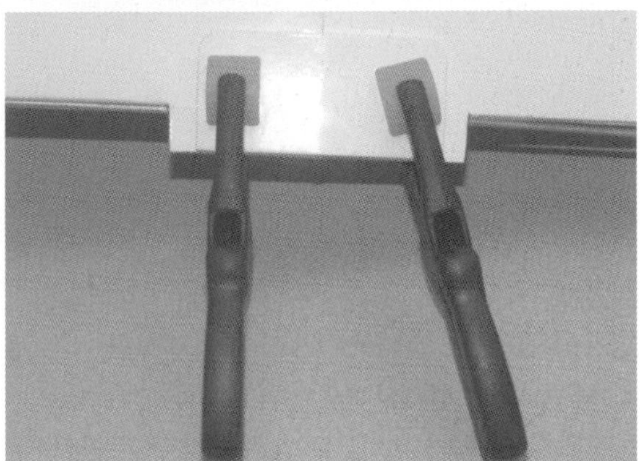

Before the rear wing mounting plate can be glued in position the film must be removed over the area to be glued, score and bend the plate, hold in position with clamps while the glue is drying.

days of sketchy instructions, written in poor English, are gone, but the standards are still variable and examples from the Far Eastern kits can leave a lot to be desired. Cost of the kit is not necessarily a guide to the quality of the instructions, some of the inexpensive models have excellent instruction manuals and the more expensive products may have poorly written, or translated instructions. Where a manufacturer has a range of kits he may try to adapt the instructions from one model to another, with as few alterations to the text as possible. There is little point of having a 40 page instruction manual if some of the vital points, dimensions of the pushrods, or disposition of the servos for instance, are left out and this can happen. If you read the instructions and are still left baffled, go back to the model shop retailer and explain your difficulties. Another good reason for buying from a reputable dealer rather than buying on-line. Sometimes the manual will give a contact number to 'phone if you have any queries, although this is often situated in the USA. If only the importers/distributors would build the model, check out the instructions and include an addendum sheet with the kits it would save every purchaser of that kit from having to overcome the same problems and errors.

The biggest problem you may come across is likely to be discrepancies between the instructions and the actual facts of the model -

Accessory contents will vary from kit to kit, some will include a spinner, some may not include wheels. Make a thorough check of the contents, to ensure they are complete and also to make a note of any additional items you may require.

usually covered by such wording as "The manufacturers reserve the right to improve and alter the contents of this kit." These discrepancies are usually of a minor nature, for instance, it may say that you have to fix the engine mount to the bulkhead and you find that it is already fitted, or the wheels are pre-fitted to the undercarriage. If a more serious alteration is required, security of the wing panels, for instance, there will usually be an addendum sheet drawing your attention to this modification. It should be remembered that the instructions will have been printed, in bulk, at the time of the first production batch of the kits and genuine improvements may be made during the life of the kit which are not reflected in the instructions. Instructions on how to fly the model are less likely to be included in the manual. It is more likely that there will be warnings about the dangers of using tools, adhesives, operating the engine and flying in general, this is to help indemnify the manufacturers from irresponsible use by the purchaser. More likely is advice to contact a local model aircraft club, or at least an experienced R/C flyer and obtain some instruction from a responsible person. This is entirely sensible advice and will avoid costly and dangerous situations, you will learn about obtaining insurance and where and where not it is permitted to fly, plus some of the basic rules of the air. In the UK we are all governed by the Air Navigation Order rules whether we fly models or full-size aircraft.

Assembly and Testing

I do not always agree with the order of assembly suggested in the manuals e.g. I prefer to fit the engine before the tail surfaces as there is quite a lot of moving and turning of the fuselage when the engine is being fitted and the tail surfaces are prone to damage. However, for the beginner it is essential to follow the instruction manual precisely and in the order recommended. Going your own way may result in you 'building-out' some important component through taking the wrong order. Always read through the instructions thoroughly

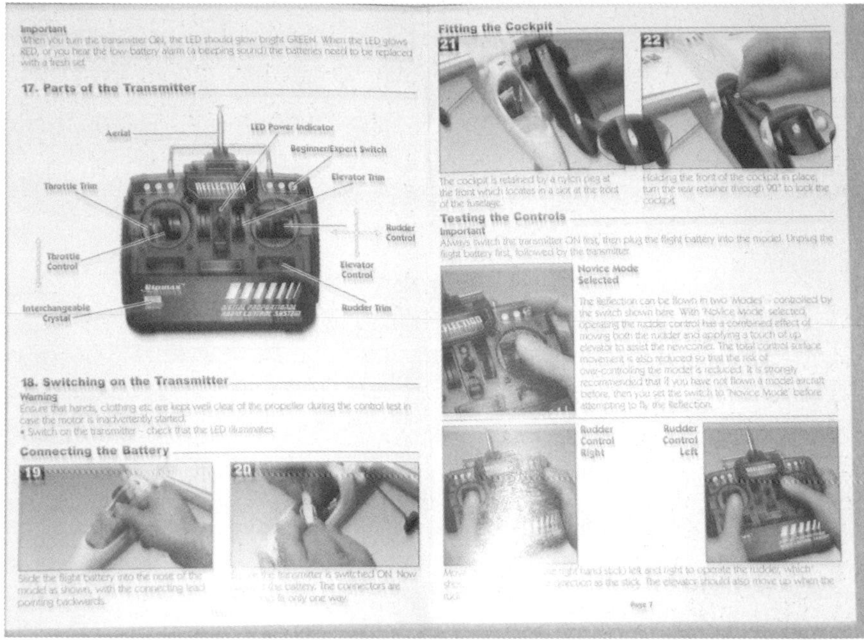
Important
When you turn the transmitter ON, the LED should glow bright GREEN. When the LED glows RED, or you hear the low battery alarm (a beeping sound) the batteries need to be replaced with a fresh set.

17. Parts of the Transmitter

18. Switching on the Transmitter

Warning

Connecting the Battery

Fitting the Cockpit

Testing the Controls

Important

Novice Mode Selected

Rudder Control Right

Rudder Control Left

The quality and content of ARTF instructions are ever improving but, if you are unsure of any part of the text or illustrations, re-read until you understand the procedures - or ask an experienced modeller.

before you commence the assembly of the model and ensure that you understand the meaning of the instructions - if not, ask!

Installation of the radio control equipment i.e. the receiver, servos, battery, switch etc., is covered by a combination of the radio control equipment manual and that of the model kit. Servo mounting plates are frequently pre-fitted, with openings pre-cut, but not all 'standard' servos are precisely the same size and you may have to increase the opening size to obtain a good fit. Alternatively, use the servos illustrated in the model manual. If it is possible to allow for alternative battery locations this could be an advantage when it comes to balancing the model. The switch location may be internal, with a wire pushrod to outside the fuselage to activate it, or mounted on the fuselage side sheeting; where the latter is the case make sure that it is positioned on the opposite side to the silencer, oil and electrics don't mix. Obviously, you must check that all the servos and control surfaces, are moving in the correct direction, but it is equally important that the linkages and surfaces move smoothly, without binding or 'slop', unwanted free movement.

Control movement deflections will be quoted in the manual, the beginner should err towards the lower end of any stated range. If the transmitter features rates you can set up the maximum recommended movements on high rate and the minimum on low rate.

Balancing

With the model completely assembled we have one final, vitally important check to make before we can contemplate flying, finding the balance point and correcting it if necessary.

Measurements for the desired balance point will be quoted in terms of 'X' inches, or millimetres from the leading edge of the wing. Put some thin strips of self-adhesive coloured tape on the underside of the wing, either side of the fuselage, at these dimensions. The temptation is then to place your fingers on these marks and lift the model in the air to see whether the model holds

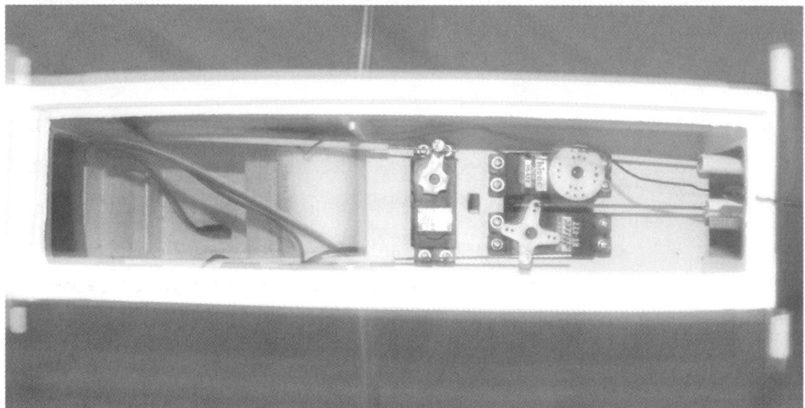

A sound and neat installation of the battery, receiver and servos is essential for reliable flying, you may have to experiment with the location of the equipment to obtain the best positions with regard to the balance of the model - and you may have to add ballast to the nose, or tail, to achieve the correct balance.

level; this is a most imprecise method and can give totally unreliable results. It is easy enough to make a balancing frame by placing two dowels into a baseboard, the tops of the dowels are chisel edge shaped and these are placed, chisel edges spanwise, on the balance marks. If you are lucky the model will balance correctly, but more likely it will be nose or tail heavy and require some ballasting. Tail heavy is the more likely situation and our first consideration should be to move the battery further forward. It may be possible to relocate it above, or below the fuel tank, but ensure that it is protected by foam and that it can be removed again, a cord fixed around the battery will help here. If it is impossible to obtain the correct balance, which should leave the model in a slightly nose down attitude (as in the glide) by moving the battery you will have to resort to adding ballast. Car wheel balancing weights are available from garages, consist of strips of 5 and 10 gram self adhesive weights and these are ideal for positioning at the front or rear of the fuselage internally. The importance of the correct balance point (also referred to as C of G, centre of gravity) cannot be over emphasised. To attempt to fly with a rearward, tail heavy location, will almost certainly end in disaster through having an uncontrollable model. With a nose heavy situation you may not even be able to persuade the model to become airborne.

Weights of the completed model, quoted in the manual or on the box lid, can be optimistic and

your example may turn out to be heavier. This will certainly be the case if ballast has been added to obtain the correct balance, but under no circumstances should the ballast be removed in an attempt to achieve the quoted A.U.W. (All Up Weight). Heavier models will still fly, albeit a little faster; out of balance models are likely to crash.

How to fly instructions

As stated, many of the beginner kits do not include any instructions on how to learn to fly the model, simply relying on the advice to join a local club or group. Not all manufacturers take this line, some will tell you to get experienced assistance and then, ambiguously, detail how to set up the model and fly it yourself. I am sometimes countered with the argument that, "if you learned to fly on your own, why can't I?" The big difference is that when I learned to fly R/C models

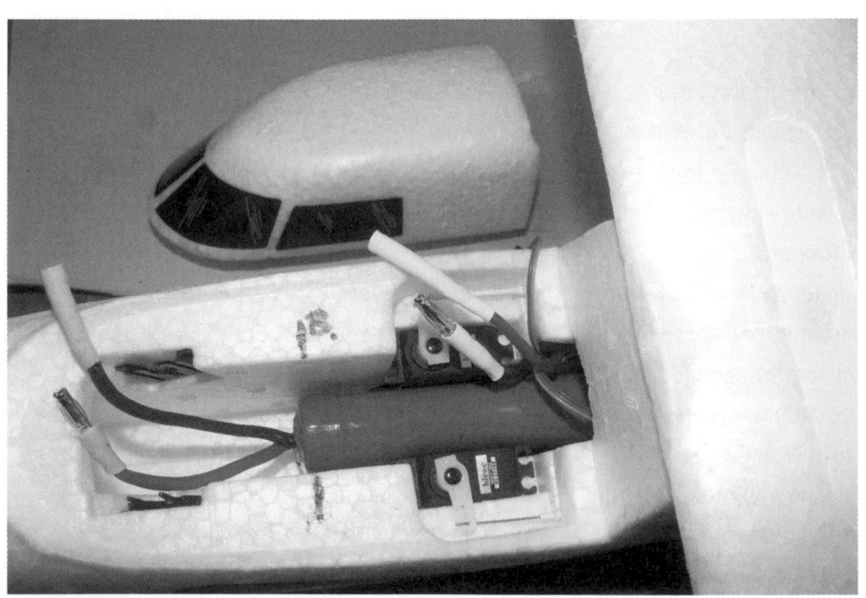

A simple balancer can be made by chisel shaping the ends of two dowels, secured in a stand (above). With electric models the location of the battery should be marked to ensure that it is correctly repositioned after removal (left).

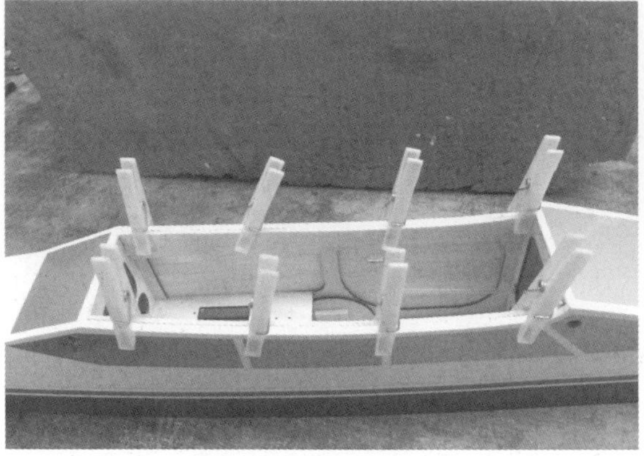

Improvements can be made to models, examples include increasing the thickness of the wing seating, adding wing seating foam tape and fitting a restrainer onto the aerial.

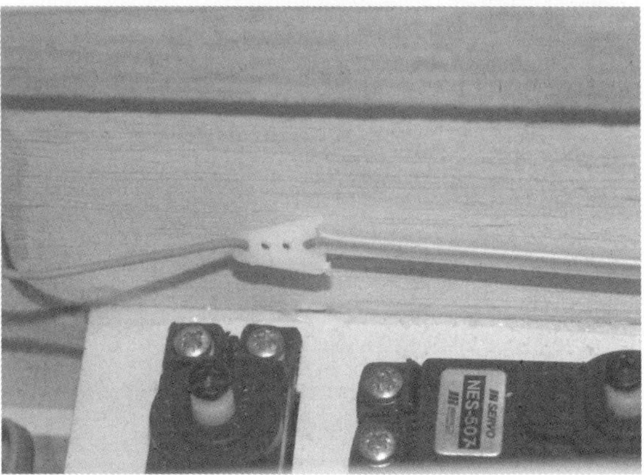

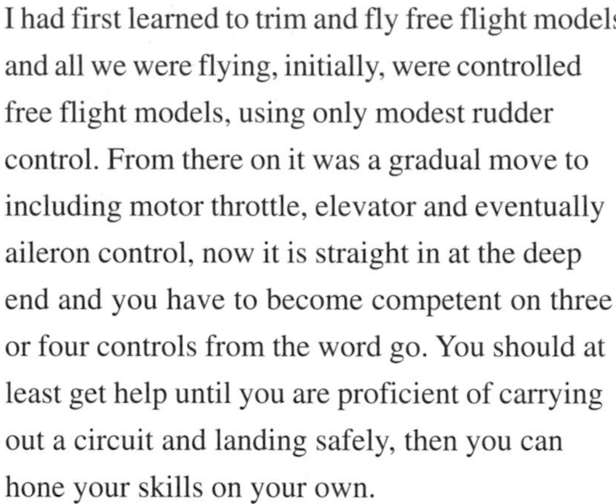

I had first learned to trim and fly free flight models and all we were flying, initially, were controlled free flight models, using only modest rudder control. From there on it was a gradual move to including motor throttle, elevator and eventually aileron control, now it is straight in at the deep end and you have to become competent on three or four controls from the word go. You should at least get help until you are proficient of carrying out a circuit and landing safely, then you can hone your skills on your own.

What about the would be R/C flyer living in a remote rural area where no assistance, other than a non-modelling, but sensible, colleague is available? In these cases I would suggest starting with an EP glider with three functions, rudder, elevator and speed controller for motor. These can be flown with low cost electric motors, speed controllers and batteries, are easy to launch, fairly stable and provided you keep to basic rules, should get you airborne in calm weather conditions. An alternative, EP or IC, is to choose a vintage style model which will be slow flying and give you maximum time to give the correct control movements, this would be a sensible option for the more mature modeller whose reactions have slowed slightly.

Improving the breed

Having a quality ARTF trainer does not mean that it cannot be improved when the assembly is taking place. Although labour is cheap in the countries of origin of the ARTF's it is still a consideration and time spent by ourselves in one or two areas can result in a greater longevity of the model. Because this preventative medicine applies to many of the ARTF models, not just trainers, the recommendations are dealt with in Chapter 6.

Summary

At a very early stage you will have to decide which direction to take with your R/C trainer model, whether it is to be a traditional IC powered

There are now many alternative types of models to start you on the road to R/C model flying, but sensible selection will, if not guarantee success, at least give you every chance of becoming a competent pilot. Choose the conventional models either IC powered or electric and be advised and assisted by experienced modellers

model, an electric version, a glider, or even to concentrate on helicopters. This is one of the most important decisions you will make so don't rush it, if you can pay a visit to a model aircraft club do so, talk to the members, ask a few questions on their preferences and what the limitations of the club are, it may be that they can only fly E.P. models because of noise restrictions. Ask, also, whether the club or group have a training scheme for beginners, this could save you a lot of anguish - and money!

Learning with electric

Why hasn't there been a direct EP trainer model equivalent to the IC standard trainer? Small electric motors, speed controllers and the batteries to power them are very economically priced, but they are only suitable for smaller sizes of models. When you are looking for more powerful motors, with specialist ESCs and large capacity batteries the costs escalate disproportionally. In the past the additional weight penalty of EP was offset by building lighter airframes, but this is not desirable for trainer models where a certain degree of ruggedness is needed. There are good compromises where both moulded foam and traditionally constructed airframes have been allied to lower cost, canned electric motors and NiCad, or NiMh batteries to good effect.

As the prices of the brushless motors, speed controllers and compatible batteries have tumbled trainer kits can be designed to reflect these improved economies and both moulded plastic and open frame models of larger wing spans can be manufactured and sold at competitive prices. These 'conventional' trainers will augment the powered glider and 'pod and boom' types and should appeal to those beginners wanting a model to represent a full-size aeroplane. Look out for these EP trainers, they will represent a good compromise between the smaller, so-called trainer

Types of foam materials have gradually improved, the Multiplex 'Easy-Star' uses a product called 'Elapor', stronger and more resilient than earlier styrofoam materials.

designs and the expensive models where the costs were prohibitive for a first model.

Moulded foam airframes and EP have proved to be a popular combination, you don't have any fuel contamination to worry about and the fitting of the motors, servos and batteries can be very simple operations. In most cases the electric motor is pre-fitted in the moulded foam fuselage and recesses are provided for the servos which are either push-fitted in place, or secured with tape or glue. Control surface hinges are frequently formed by compression of the plastic during moulding, forming a durable and reasonably free airtight hinge. If the control linkage runs are also incorporated it doesn't leave too much work to get the model to a flying state. The battery is secured with Velcro style tape and straps and the speed controller and receiver can be fixed to the internal surfaces by the same method. Exactly how much time you have to spend to get the model completely ready for flying varies considerably. For some it is a matter of minutes and others take a period of hours to reach the same stage, read the reviews, or ask the retailer for advice and choose the model to suit your fancy.

When you have considered all of the options and read the following chapters, make your decision, buy the equipment and go fly. The early learning phases can be the most enjoyable, exciting and rewarding phases of the hobby/sport - it remains debatable under which category building and flying R/C models can be classified.

Chapter 4

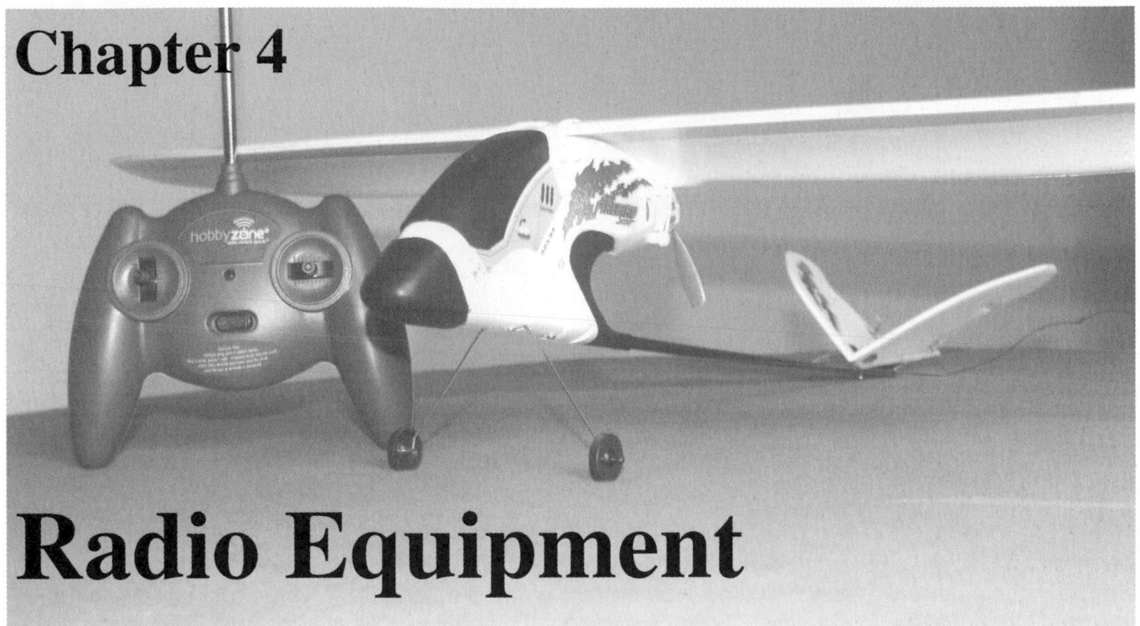

Radio Equipment

Many of the lower cost electric models are supplied complete with radio equipment at quite attractive prices. Whether these represent good buys depends on a number of factors. If you knew to what degree you were going to be involved in the hobby it would be an easy matter to advise on the radio equipment to purchase in the first instance, but how many of us are certain that we will take to the hobby seriously and stay with it for a number of years? Visiting a training school, see 'Useful Contacts' at the end of this book, and having a trial lesson is one way of getting a feel of flying R/C models, or if a local model club can provide some dual control experience, this should also give a taste of the activity. Where you have to make an independent decision there will be a temptation to go for a complete ARTF outfit, perhaps costing £100, or so, but is this the best way forward? The radio, a two or three function (functions) may be on the 27 band and some clubs will not allow this equipment to be used at their flying fields and if you try to fly it at other public areas, possibly illegally, you may suffer from interference from other R/C model operators; 27MHz is also used for model cars and boats. Even if the complete outfit you purchase is on the 35MHz band the transmitter will probably be, at the best, on four channels, without some of the more desirable operations such as dual rates, servo end point adjustments, frequency crystal changing and other functions which will, in a very short time, be considered as necessary. One other drawback with the 'complete package' deal is that the transmitter is normally supplied for dry battery operation. Non-rechargeable dry batteries are bad news for anybody contemplating a reasonable amount of flying, they are less convenient and reliable and represent poor economics as they tend to be changed, on safety grounds, more frequently than is strictly necessary. If you do decide to purchase, say, a four function EP trainer with three servos and an ESC, for around £100, ensure that it is on 35MHz and that the radio equipment is transferable to other models, also

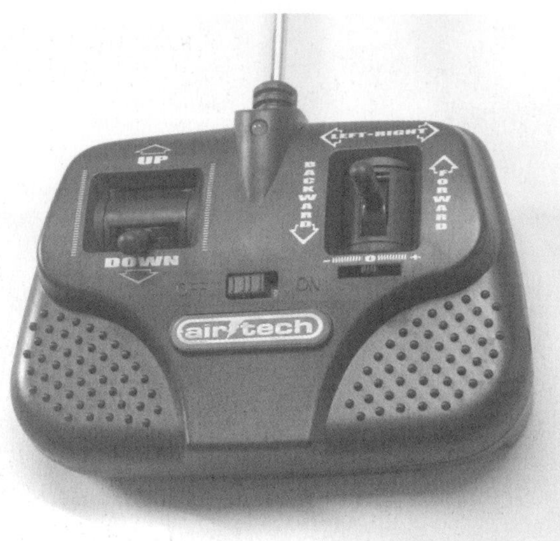

Transmitters may take different forms and styles, but they all perform the same functions. Low cost electric models normally feature two channel system or three functions, elevator, rudder and motor control. Occasionally a four function, with the addition of aileron control, is supplied.

that the transmitter has a charging socket so that you can replace the dry batteries with rechargeable ones. With such a purchase you will be able to continue using the radio for simple powered models, including IC power by purchasing an additional servo and gliders. For more advanced aerobatic and scale models you will have to invest in a more sophisticated radio system but it is no bad thing to have a back-up set, possibly installed in a small electric sports model for when you want to get in ten minutes flying on an evening when you don't want to get all the other equipment ready.

Invest in the future

For enthusiasts fairly certain that they will continue and progress in the hobby I would

Dry batteries normally power the low cost outfit transmitters, but it is wise to replace these (AA cells) with rechargeable nicad or nickel metal hydride cells as soon as possible.

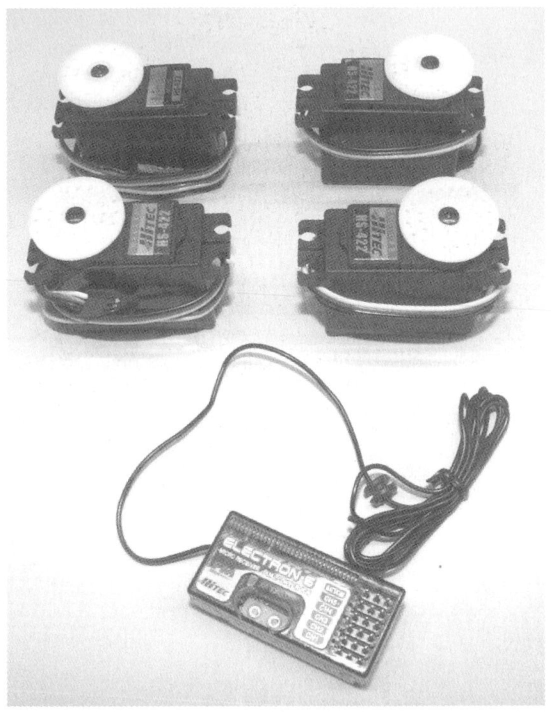

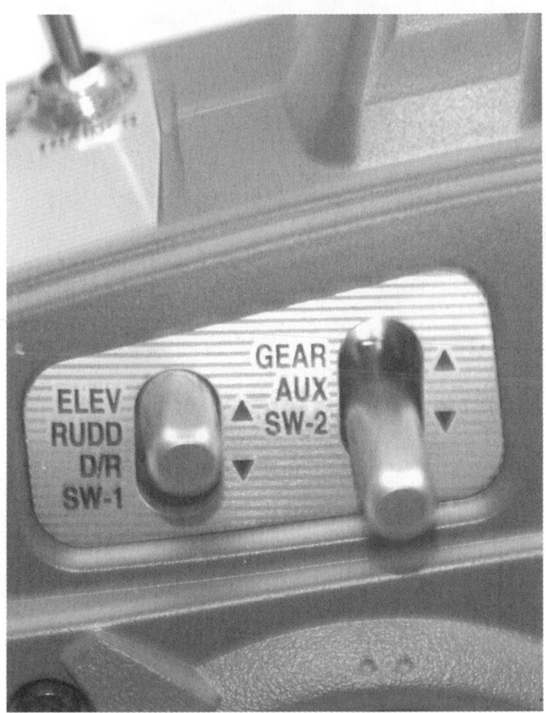

Four and six channel radio systems are normally supplied with receiver and four servos - plus batteries etc. A six channel outfit should suffice for the majority of enthusiasts, it will provide the extra functions of undercarriage retracts and flaps etc.

strongly recommend purchasing one of the entry level six function digital FM radio systems. These outfits include the transmitter, receiver, rechargeable batteries, mains charger, four servos and accessories, they include 35MHz frequency crystals and comprehensive instruction manuals. The transmitter is supplied on Mode 1, where the elevator control is on the left-hand stick, or Mode 2 where the elevator and aileron control are on the right hand stick. Which Mode to purchase? Go to your nearest club and see which Mode is predominantly used and opt for that, you may be asking for their assistance in learning to fly and operating on the same model will be helpful.

Advances in computer technology has allowed the introduction of many additional functions without the costs rising in proportion and today's entry level radio system is the equivalent of yesterday's expert outfit. Another introduction on the economy cost transmitters is the synthesised frequency module, which can be adjusted to any of the 35MHz frequencies and eliminates the need for frequency control crystals - although these are still required in the receivers.

Typical features of a six function digital FM system, which is suitable for power models, gliders and helicopters includes:-

Eight Model Memory - trim settings etc. are stored for each model

Four Character Model Naming - on the screen to indicate the model to be flown

Model Copy - transferring of a memory to another transmitter

Two Programmable Mixers - for instance, rudder

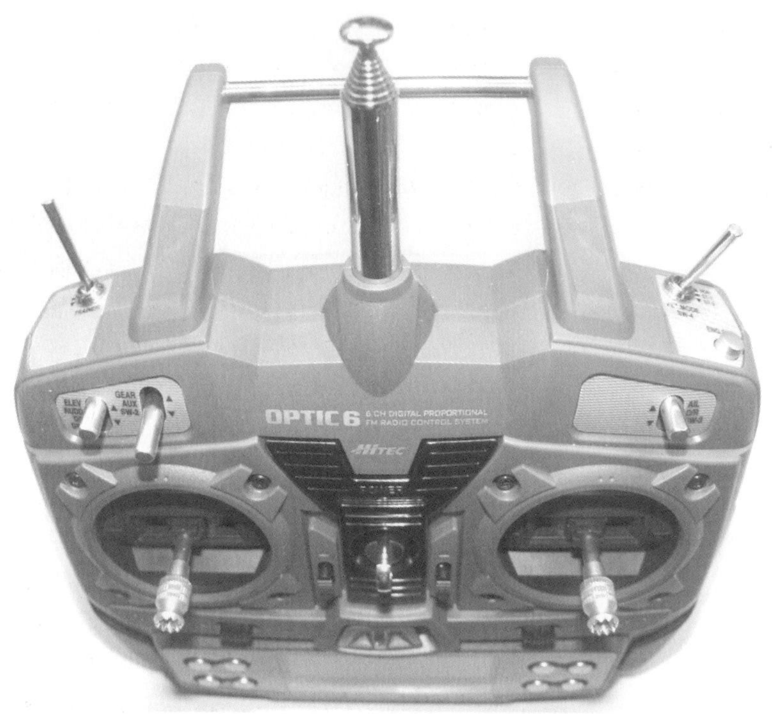

The functions provided by a six channel system are listed in the text; most of the auxiliary function switches are located on the top of the transmitter. Synthesised frequency control, giving access to the complete frequency range, is possible by a unit, which is plugged into the rear of the transmitter, see below.

and aileron mixing

Dual Timer - showing flight time and power run time

EPA - end point adjustment on all channels

Servo Reversing - on all channels

Dual Rates - on at least aileron and elevator channels

Exponential Rates - on rudder, aileron and elevator

Trainer Jack - to facilitate a dual control system

For helicopter flying there are open mixes, gyro gain, pitch curves, revo mix and CCPM mixing.

PCM (Pulse Code Modulation) signal may be available in addition to FM (Frequency Modulation) this could be an advantage when moving onto larger models where fail-safe operations are a priority, although this facility may

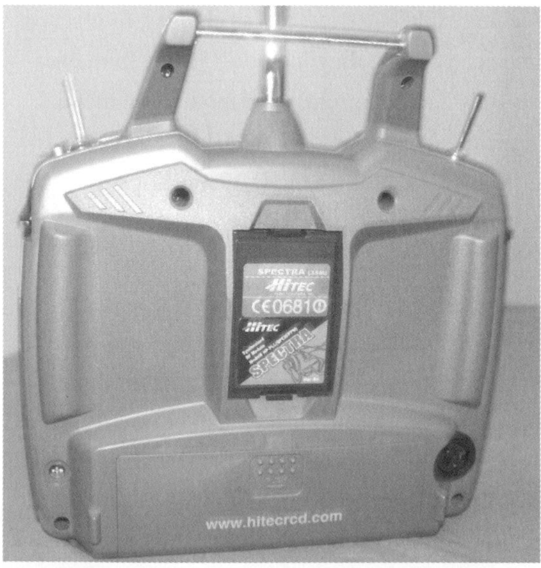

also be available on some FM systems.
From here onwards the radio systems have more functions available, more programmable features, more model memories, until you reach the top of the range systems which may have 14 functions and fully automated frequency searching where the transmitter and receiver will lock onto a free frequency, but only operate on that frequency after it is given a command to do so. There are dangers in synthesised frequency searching where the transmitter automatically operates on a free frequency. Unless the frequency control system being operated by the club is immediately put into operation e.g. a frequency peg of the appropriate frequency is placed on the board, there is a real chance that two transmitters on the same frequency may be switched on at the same time. It will be many years before all of the radio systems have automated synthesised frequency control.

Model aircraft R/C flyers have not always been restricted to the 27 and 35MHz bands for their radio systems, for a time equipment on the UHF (Ultra High Frequency) frequencies from 458.525 to 495.475MHz was produced. It was very successful as far as operation was concerned and it was less susceptible to interference from outside sources. The only apparent reason for its demise was that it cost more to produce and was not competitive against the FM and PCM systems on the 35MHz band. It continues to be used for military purposes where cost is less of a consideration.

For close range flying, with small helicopters, electric mini-3D and indoor style models a new system is coming onto the market. Operating on the 2.4GHz spectrum it neither affects the 27 and 35MHz bands, nor is it affected by their transmissions. The equipment i.e. transmitter, receiver, servos etc. is of conventional appearance, it is the operation of the system that differs. By employing two of the 2.4GHz band's 80 functions in a unique formation it delivers a redundant RF link to the model, irrespective of its orientation. When the transmitter is switched on it automatically searches for two clear functions and locks onto these and becomes immune to interference from other 2.4GHz band users, or other forms of interference. At the time of writing (2006) the equipment is awaiting testing and approval in the UK. Read the model magazines for updates on this promising system.

When your R/C system does not have synthesised frequency options and they are by no means the norm, it would be sensible to have a word with the model club members, if you are going to join a club, to see the best frequency to choose. Some clubs try to dedicate spot frequencies to individual members, some only operate on even, or odd numbers and some retain parts of the frequency band for specific models e.g. gliders. It is, therefore, important to know the frequency limitations, if any, before buying your outfit. Even if there are not specific restrictions it may be that there is a preponderance of usage of certain frequencies and it would be best to avoid selecting these.

Adding to the system

Having purchased your R/C outfit you might be excused from believing that is the end of the matter, but it certainly is not. The four servos supplied with the outfit will be of standard size and output type, perfectly adequate for trainer and sports models, but not the best for high power models, helicopters, 3D and micro models. For these models there is a vast range of servos, one manufacturer lists over 50, ranging from the

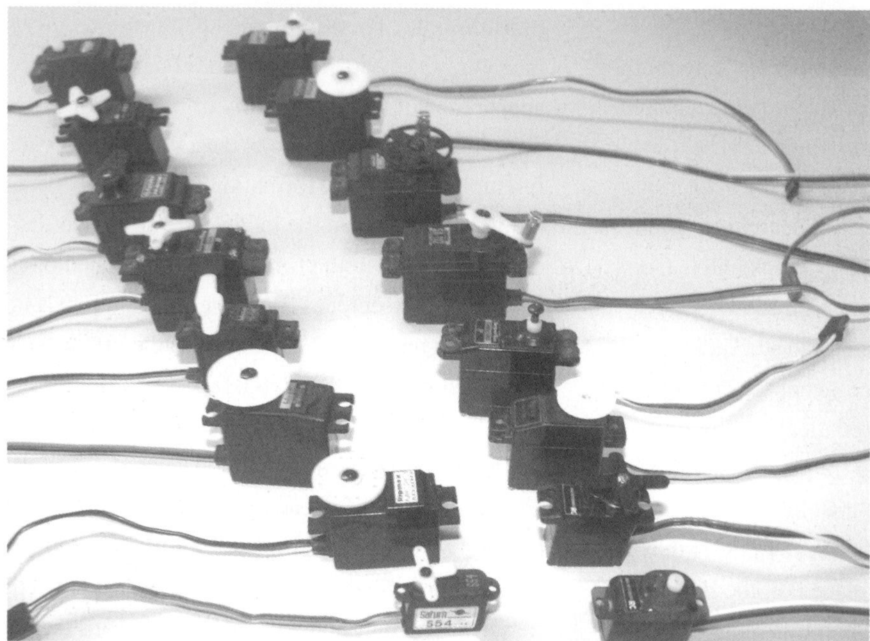

Servos come in all forms of outputs, sizes and weights, also speeds of operation. Your selection will depend on the model type and the accuracy of control required.

smallest, weighing only a couple of grams, to the high torque, high speed servos with titanium alloy gear trains. Of course, you only need to buy these additional servos as they are needed for a particular project, fortunately they will be compatible with the original six-function radio system. Similarly, it is possible to buy additional receivers from micro sizes to larger types in various shapes. Only FM receivers can be operated by non-PCM transmitters and these will be either single or dual conversion, the latter being less suspect to inter-function interference.
It is vital to purchase the correct type of crystal for the receiver i.e. single or dual conversion of the same manufacture as the receiver. The transmitter crystal remains the same irrespective of the type of receiver being used; it just has to be on the same frequency.
When you move on to larger and more powerful models you will need larger receiver/servo batteries and conversely a smaller battery for micro models. It is also most likely that you will need servo extension leads (when the servos are at a distance from the receiver) and a 'Y' lead where separate servos are used for the ailerons; although it should also be possible to use two separate outlets from the receiver and programme the transmitter to operate the individual aileron servos in the correct orientation.
Unless you rapidly move on to complex models, such as scale designs with retracting undercarriages, flaps, bomb dropping etc., or competition standard aerobatic and 3D models, the 6 function FM Computer outfit should cope with your needs for a long time. Yes, you will probably add receivers, servos, switches etc. to fit into other models, to avoid having to move them around from one model to another, but the transmitter can be common to all models - until you have more than eight fully equipped models and you run out of model memories! By the time you reach this blissful state you will know enough about R/C model aircraft and equipment to make your own decision about future purchases.

Chapter 5

Electric Power

From a time when advocates of electric power for R/C model aircraft pretended that it was the equivalent in power to weight ratios to IC engine powered models - and it wasn't - we are now at the stage where EP is certainly the equal in performance to those with glo motors. In some instances the EP models may outperform their IC powered brethren, but this may only come at a financial cost and a need to treat the specialist batteries with considerable care. For most of us and for the purpose of this book we will not be considering the most powerful motors, or the highest capacity lithium batteries and chargers, these are for the more experienced EP modellers; there are enough decisions to be made by the newcomer without having more alternatives to consider.

The rapidity of developments in EP equipment is quite staggering and it continues to amaze. It is not only in the specifications and efficiencies of motors, speed controllers and batteries that great advances have been made, but in the costs of the equipment, too. What was the plaything of the rich is now affordable by the 'ordinary' modellers, which is admirable but does render equipment obsolete and worthless in very short order. I believe that we have now reached a stage where the modeller can purchase the latest equipment and not have to worry about it being totally superseded in a short time. Of course there will be further developments and improvements, but not to the degree we have seen with the introduction of brushless motors and lithium polymer batteries. It is also true to say that some of the older technology, using brushed motors and NiMh batteries is perfectly adequate for certain types of models, it is only when extra performance is required, or larger, faster models that the newer technology is essential.

What types of models are suitable for EP? The simple answer is any that are also suited to IC power, again with the proviso that the costs may be greater and the technology more complicated. In the field of ARTF models the aircraft kitted will be designed for electric power or IC engines,

although a few can utilise either and the requirements will be clearly stated on the kit box, or in the advertisements. What are the advantages of EP? Apart from the obvious ones of cleanliness and quietness (they are not silent as there is some mechanical noise and propeller noise) there are other benefits. Not all modellers are of a mechanical bent and may find the starting and setting of an IC engine difficult. With an electric motor starting is instantaneous and it is also unlikely that the motor will stop unless instructed to from the transmitter, or due to the battery running out of power. This is a reassuring benefit and none more so than with multi-engine models.

Variety is the spice of life and variety is what you get with electric power ARTF models, if it flies, it will be represented by an EP model.

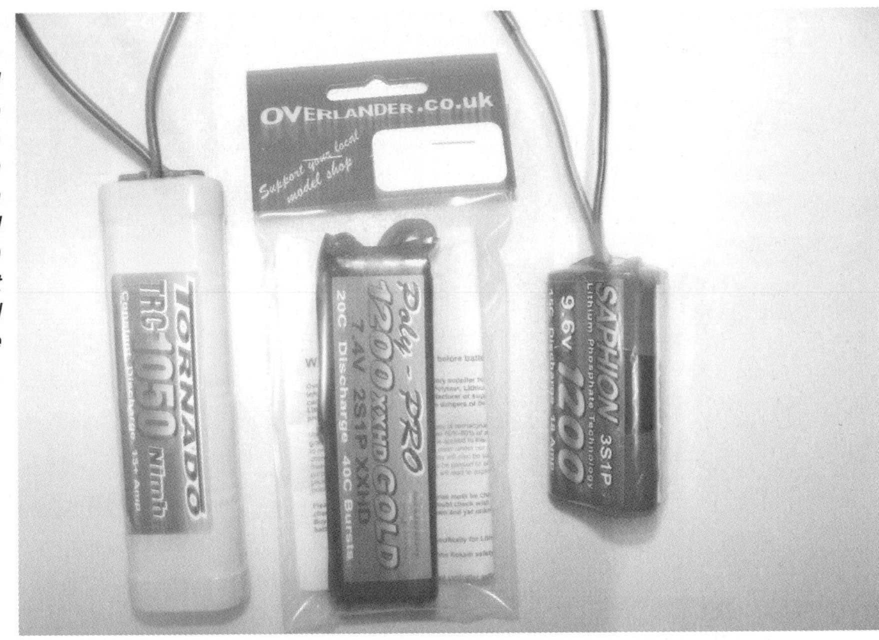

Batteries for EP take the form of NiMh (Nickel Metal Hydride), LiPo (Lithium Polymer) and Saphion (Lithium Phosphate) as seen on the left. Nicad (Nickel Cadmium) are still popular, but are due to be phased out because of the cadmium content.

At some time throughout their involvement with the hobby, the enthusiast is likely to wish to build a scale model of a World War Two aircraft, often a Supermarine Spitfire, but also twin engined types such as the D.H. Mosquito. As an IC powered model the Mosquito is a tricky subject because if one engine fails, or loses power, there is a difficult unbalanced situation where the good engine is tending to turn the model into the dead one. It may be possible to retrieve the situation by applying opposite rudder to the direction of the turn, or by closing the throttle of the good engine, but if the model is at distance these are not easy options and the model may have flicked into a spin before you have had time to react. With electric motors this situation is unlikely to occur and if power is cut by the BEC (Battery Eliminator Circuit) system because of lowering battery state, it will be to both engines and not just one.

Claims that EP is better because you don't have to carry so much equipment to the flying area is only partially true. Certainly you don't have to take fuel, a starter, glo battery etc., but you do have to lug around a hefty 12V battery to recharge the batteries for the model. If expense is no consideration you could take four or five fully charged batteries to use in the model, but this is poor economics in initial expense; a further advantage of EP is the low cost of supplying the energy, mains electricity is a lot cheaper than glo fuel.

Where to start

As this is a book about ARTF's the obvious advice is to purchase a 'package deal' with the motor, ESC, receiver and servos pre-fitted. This would be sound advice as you don't have to worry about matching motors with propellers, speed controllers and batteries, it is ready sorted. However, you will, at some time, want to progress to the stage where you may still purchase an ARTF airframe, but wish to fit it out with electric equipment purchased separately. You will probably build a stock of motors, speed controllers and batteries, also propellers, with a view to fitting them in a variety of models, in the same way that IC

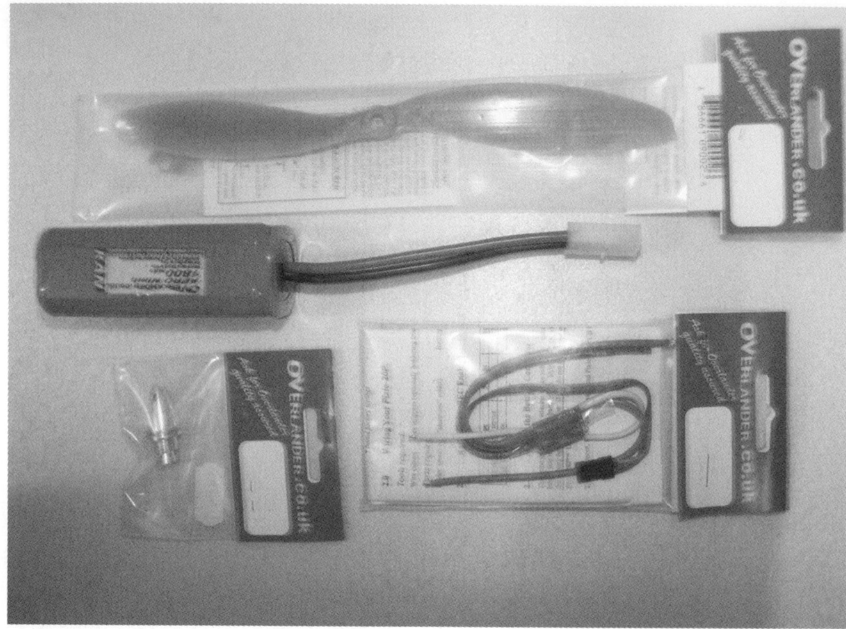

It is important to have a fully matched EP system i.e. motor, speed controller, battery and propeller, if the equipment is not sold as a set be advised by the specialist retailer on the items you will require for your project.

motors may be transferred from model to model. In order to do that you will need a basic knowledge of electronics, or at least how your equipment works and how to select the products.

In very basic terms the EP installation consists of a battery which supplies power to the motor, it may also, by means of a BEC provide power to the receivers, the latter taking preference when the battery power begins to fade. In addition there will be an ESC to control the current to the electric motor. Now it starts to get more complicated.

I am indebted to Over-tec for the following comments taken from their catalogue, it is a mine of information:

Advances in EP make it possible to fly helicopters and micro fixed wing model aircraft in the comfort of your lounge.

Power pack voltage

The first decision for electric flight is whether to use 7.2, 8.4 or 9.6V.

In general terms always use 8.4V, though the pack is heavier everything else works in your favour. The extra power comfortably compensates for the weight, but perhaps unexpectedly the higher voltage also gives longer running times when used with BEC (battery eliminator circuits) on speed controls, i.e. the average BEC cuts in at 5V, on a 7.2V pack. That is 0.84V per cell, as against 0.71V per cell. this typically gives 20% longer running time. Also it is interesting to note that 8.4V packs can be charged on 7.2V chargers, they just take a little longer, 9.6V packs do need their own charger.

Do you understand milliamps?

Look at it this way, you see Rx packs for instance with 500mAh or 600mAh or more written on them. Think of them as 30 or 40 litre etc. fuel tanks, i.e. the larger the number the longer the running time, it does not mean that the pack is necessarily any more powerful. In fact quite often the higher the mAh in the same size of cell can mean it is less powerful. It is like comparing a sprinter with a marathon runner, the bigger number will run for ever but does not pack the punch. So the big number is great for transmitters and receivers, but it is not always the best for motor running.

Remember to get more out you have to put more in, i.e. you have to charge for longer, or charge at a higher rate. Formula for charging empty packs:-

1) Add 20% to value of capacity, i.e. 800mAh becomes 960mAh

2) Divide by charger output, if you have a 60mAh charger it will take 16 hours to charge the above.

Charging

Generally do not 'Autocharge' cells other than sub 'C' type or greater in size, you may get away with many charges, but cyclic life of your pack will be greatly reduced.

The first charge should always be a timed charge at a rate at near to 10% of the capacity for 12-14 hours. Never 'peak detect' the first charge, as the cells are not yet 'formed' or 'conditioned', and undercharging or overcharging can and **will occur**. Discharge your packs before giving a full charge.

It is good practice to cycle your packs a couple of times before using, and to check voltage and capacity regularly. Do not rely on a battery checker unless it is specifically calibrated to your battery pack. Using hot packs straight off the charger for electric flight is okay, but **LET THEM COOL BEFORE RECHARGING**. Take care with nickel metal hydride cell charging, technology has given us some great cells with massive capacity; patience during a little longer charging time being the only down side.

The advice to use extended charging rates, as opposed to rapid charging, cannot be over emphasised, it will greatly extend the life of the cells and it is the safer option.

Nothing's for nothing

Whether you want a short, flat out, powerful aerobatic flight, or a more docile, cruising performance of longer duration will determine the battery you choose; we need to consider power (volts V) and capacity (milliamps mAh).

Power is controlled by the number of cells in the pack; i.e. more cells, more volts, more power.

Think of capacity, as the size of the fuel tank. This is where it gets weird for most modellers, as cells with the same physical size can have different capacities, and the biggest capacity will certainly have the longest duration, but not the power. Consider this, have you ever bought a car for the size of its fuel tank? (think milliamps) probably not, but you would consider the cubic capacity (think Volts here) and the number of cylinders (think cells). Too often battery capacity is confused with power. Why are larger capacity cells not as powerful as lower capacity cells of the same size? In a nutshell the higher the capacity, the denser the electrolyte, this means also that the cells internal resistance will be higher. Think of it like this; 30 passengers can alight from a bus far more quickly than 50 passengers on the same size bus, if 50 passengers try to get off the bus in the same time as 30 they would cause a jam at the door. With a battery you do not get a jam, but the voltage collapses - no volts, no power.

Battery types

Enough of theory, what about the types of batteries for EP models? For many years the NiCad cells have been the automatic choice and these rechargeable batteries were gradually improved in respect of power to weight ratios. It now seems likely that, because of the cadmium content, the NiCads will be phased out, fortunately we have alternatives.

NiMh batteries are both more eco-friendly and efficient than Nicads so, at a little extra cost we have an excellent replacement. Initially their discharge rates were more limited, but this is no longer the case and recharging does not present any special problems. For the majority of R/C model aircraft flying i.e. unless you need maximum power, or very extended flight times, the NiMh batteries will serve you well. With the same 1.2V nominal per cell as the NiCad and with an excellent safety record, they are available in a wide range of capacities, sizes and configurations for transmitters and airborne packs.

Lithium Polymer (LiPo) batteries

The introduction of LiPo cells gave the first quantum power increase from batteries for model aircraft, it also brought many misunderstandings and dangers for the uninformed. Tales of LiPo battery packs catching fire, in models and during charging and even of cells exploding started to circulate, causing concern through the modelling world. Why was it that LiPo batteries could be used in cameras and other electrical equipment with absolute impunity, but real dangers were apparent in our operation of the batteries? The problems were occurring because of the power rating of the early batteries, we were trying to take too much out of the batteries, too quickly, or charging at too high a rate, over-heating the cells, possibly leading to a conflagration. LiPo cells have improved enormously, not only in the 'C' ratings, but also in the manufacturing standards where the spacing of the cells and quality of the collector plates and terminals are more suited to our, fairly brutal usage.

LiPo batteries are normally supplied with good instructions on their care and operation, but you may be purchasing them second hand and need to know more about them. Puffin Models Ltd. put out a very comprehensive sheet explaining the Do's and Don't s of LiPo batteries, it may seem to be a long list of dire warnings, it is not intended to frighten the prospective user, but to give sound advice to prevent accidents and is reproduced in full as follows:

"Warning: This sheet contains vital information on the safe use of Lithium Polymer batteries. Be sure to read it carefully before you even touch Lithium Polymer (Lipo) cells or batteries for the first time.

Lithium Polymer (LiPo) battery packs offer the modeller high capacity with low weight. Because of the nature of Lithium Polymer cells they

require careful selection for use and careful handling. 1C is the 1 hour rate for the cells. 1C for a 1000mAh pack is 1A, and 10C is 10A.
All lithium cells from all manufacturers lose capacity with use. The loss in capacity is related to the current drawn from the pack. When used at up to 5C, lithium cells can last for up to 1000 cycles. When used at 10C, E-Tec HP lithium polymer cells will lose up to 10% of capacity after 100 cycles. We suggest buying packs with a good reserve of capacity for long service life.
Warning: Charging a Lithium battery using a charger intended for Nickel Cadmium (NiCad) or Nickel Metal Hydride (NiMH) cells can lead to a violent chemical reaction.
Please follow these do's and don'ts for successful use of lithium polymer batteries:
Allow lithium batteries to cool fully before re-charging.
Charge lithium batteries at no faster than the 1C rate.
Only use a charger with a dedicated programme for lithium batteries.
Charge lithium batteries at no more than 4.2V per cell.
Only charge a lithium battery on a non-conducting and non-inflammable surface.
Only charge lithium batteries outside.
Always monitor lithium batteries during charging.
Only use lithium battery packs as supplied by the manufacturer.
Store lithium batteries in a part charged state and out of reach of children, always keep out of reach of any person who has not read this manual or refuses to follow the instructions.
If a lithium battery becomes damaged, the battery should be monitored outside as it could then be a fire risk.
Store and dispose of any suspect battery outside.
Always use a speed controller suitable for lithium batteries for brushless motors, or brushed motors.
Always land your model when the power starts to reduce.
Never charge lithium batteries inside a house, car, model, or near inflammable material.
Never use a charger that does not have the facility to confirm the number of lithium cells before charging is started.
Never overcharge lithium cells.
Never store lithium batteries in a car or other container which may get hot.
Never modify lithium battery packs.
Never discharge lithium batteries below 3V per cell (measured off load).
Never puncture a lithium cell.
Never short circuit a lithium cell.
Never touch the contents of a lithium cell.
If you have any questions at all about the responsible use of lithium polymer battery packs please do contact your supplier.
Copyright 2005 Puffin Models Limited."

Nominal voltage of LiPo cells is 3.7Vs and battery packs consist of two or more cells; they are specified with the mAh capacity and the power rating e.g. 20C, 2500mAh, 11.1V 50amp, or 20 3S 1p 2,500mAh (the same battery) regrettably there is no standardisation in specification, as yet. With such confusing definitions as 2S-8.4v and 3/1 2000P-CS you would do well to consult your supplier before buying. When you get into the world of cells arranged in parallel and individual cell peak charging you will, or should have plenty of experience in dealing with LiPo batteries, chargers and ESC's.

Lithium-Ion

Less well known, but likely to increase in popularity, are the Lithium based cells using different chemicals to the LiPo cobalt dioxide mixes, such as the Saphion Power cell Lithium Phosphate

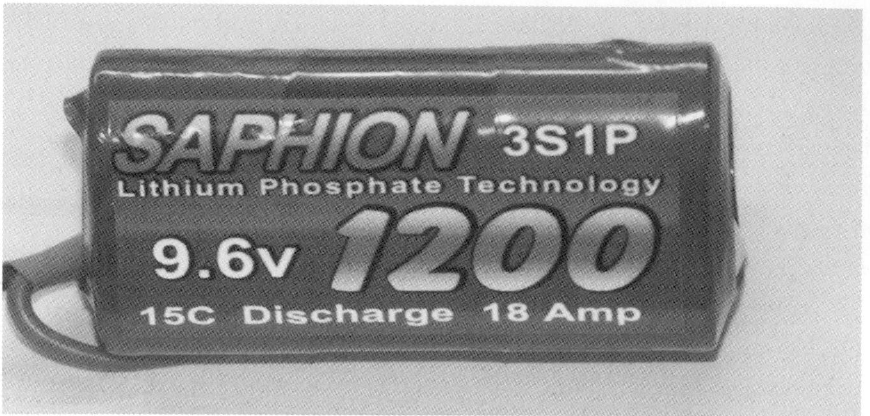

Lithium Phosphate and Lithium Ion batteries have not found particular favour with modellers, but they do have certain advantages over Nicad and NiMh cells and are less critical in charging than LiPo batteries.

based cells. Lacking the absolute power to weight ratios of the LiPo's these cells have a number of other advantages which makes them attractive to the less technically minded modellers. It is virtually impossible to overcharge the Saphion Power cell batteries, you can run them down to low voltages without causing damage and they will recharge. They have excellent voltage stability, the nominal voltage per cell is 3.2Vs, a three cell pack is the direct equivalent to an eight cell NiMh pack. Standard chargers can be used, it is possible to charge at a high rate, but this is likely to be detrimental to the life of the cells.

No doubt there will be further developments in the battery field regarding performance and reliability, for the newcomer it would be advisable to err on the side of safe and easy operation, leave the ultimate power sources to a later date.

Before leaving the subject of batteries, one further word of warning, never, ever be tempted to buy cheap dry batteries, the sort on offer at 20 for £1.00, they will let you down very rapidly and probably with disastrous results, the dangers of buying cheap LiPo batteries, from unknown sources should be equally obvious.

Electric Motors

For many years the brushed electric motor was the staple diet of the electric model enthusiast and thanks to the wide usage of these small motors, from anything to space vehicles and car windscreen water pumps, the prices were extremely competitive. Typical of these motors were the 380, 400 and 600 sizes, either geared or ungeared and many ARTF models still use these types. The limitations of power were not a factor for smaller sports models and if an increase of total power was required it could be obtained by coupling two motors together, with gearing, or having two or four engine designs. Brushed motors, direct drive, or geared, should not be discounted for ARTF models, they offer a low cost introduction to EP and providing you keep within the envelope of model and motor performance you will be rewarded with satisfactory flying for minimum expense.

Just as brushed motors were reaching their maximum efficiency along came a new and more efficient technology in the form of the brushless motor. Theoretically, because brushless motors are less complex than the brushed type, they should have been less expensive but that, initially, was not the case, it is only when production levels reach the millions that costs really tumble. With better power to weight ratios (an all

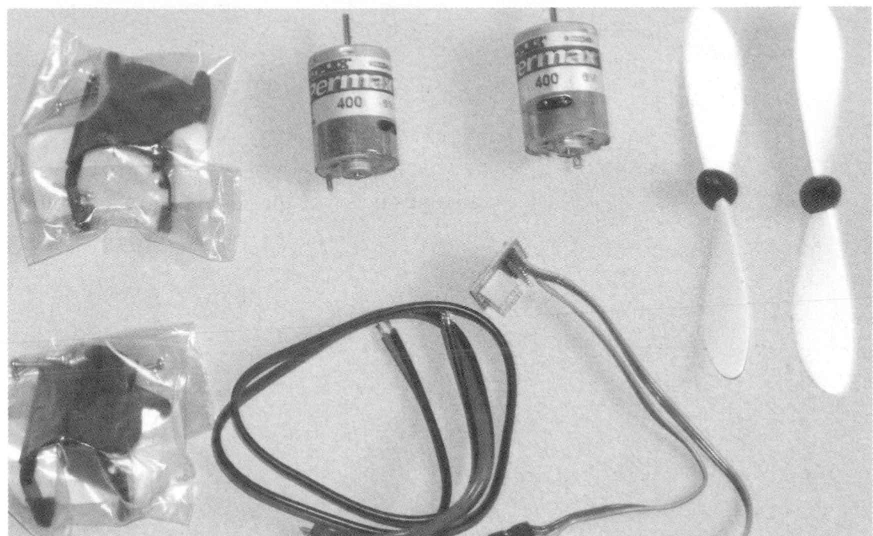

Selecting the correct motors can be a minefield, the more so because of the new types coming onto the market and cut-price offers on the Internet. It can be a case of buy in haste and regret at leisure.

important factor for heavier than air machines) the brushless motor became a popular alternative, allowing improved flight performances simply by substituting the original brushed motor with a brushless version.

Having taken the brushless motor on board there then followed a further development in the form of the outrunner motor. This is also a brushless type but, whereas with the conventional brushless motor the inner magnet rotates with the drive shaft, with the outrunner motor the magnets are bonded to the inside surface of the outer casing, which rotates with the shaft. Where the outrunner motor scores over the conventional brushed and brushless motors is that it can turn large propellers without the need to gear the outputs. Naturally, because of the rotating case, the outrunner motor requires a different mounting to the other types. Conversely, if you are looking for a high revving motor for EDF (Electric Ducted Fan) then the conventional brushless types are the answer.

Speed Controllers

Speed controllers must be matched to the type of motor being used, you will need a different ESC for brushed and brushless motors, it will also need to be of sufficient amperage to take the maximum power of the motor. Unless you are using separate battery supplies for the motor and the receiver/ servos the ESC will need a BEC circuit to provide the additional supply. Additional desirable features include dynamic braking, for ensuring folding propellers fold, soft start, safe power arming to prevent accidental start-up and, for 3D shock flyers, forward and reverse running.

Selection of EP systems is easiest at the lower end of the market, when you get to the highly sophisticated area of specialist models, such as the 3D helicopter below, you also need specialist knowledge.

Chargers

Although it is possible to purchase dedicated LiPo chargers, or specifically for Nicad and NiMh batteries it would be advisable, if you are going to be a serious advocate of electric flight, to go for a charger capable of slow and fast charging, from the mains or a 12V battery, the full range of battery types. It will prove to be more economic in the long run. Another consideration is the plugs and sockets to use for the batteries, motors and speed controllers. Tamiya style connectors are often supplied with models and equipment, but the gold plated bayonet style connectors, available in 4mm and 2mm diameter sizes, will give a consistency in fittings and enable batteries to be used in a variety of models.

There is more to electric flight, much more, with ranges of electric flight propellers, watts meters, individual cell LiPo chargers and, of course, the full range of ARTF models designed for electrics. There is much to learn, don't try to run before you can walk, get into this aspect of R/C model flying the easy way, with a full package model and expand from there. Read the modelling magazines to learn about new developments and products, there will be plenty.

Chapter 6

Easier Assembly, Preventative Maintenance and Repairs

On purchasing an ARTF kit your natural reaction is to open the box and see what goodies there are inside. Your first action should be to determine how to open the box, not the easiest of operations with some of the very clever packaging, but the last thing you want to do at this stage is to damage any of the contents. Having carefully removed the components your next operation should be to check the contents against a list in the Instruction Manual. If there are any missing parts - or you think there are some missing items - you will want to return the kit in as complete a state as possible, not easy if you have strewn the parts and packages all over the place. Another good reason, incidentally, for buying from a local dealer where it is easy to verify the contents and if necessary replace any broken components; if you do have to return the kit to a mail order, or Internet supplier they may insist that the complete package is returned, but telephone first.

Having confirmed the contents of the kit as being complete, but not having opened every small polythene packet and scattered the contents, as there may be dozens of fittings and it is advisable to keep them in groups, it is then time to read and re-read the instructions to familiarise with the order of assembly and the additional items required. At the risk of repeating myself I will warn that the instructions may not totally agree with the contents, there may have been improvements or changes made, often as a result of review comments, which are not reflected in the instructions. In a perfect world changes to the contents e.g. the servo tray being pre-fitted and not supplied separately, would be mentioned in the instructions, or an addendum, but it is not a perfect world. It does upset me when I see large, full colour, box artwork showing the completed model without an engine and silencer, or servos fitted - that is cheating. There are numerous new kit introductions, but is it too much to ask that the distributors take one from the first batch, assemble and fly it to see whether there are any potential problem areas?

Let me confirm that the comments made here are very general, many of the kits go together without

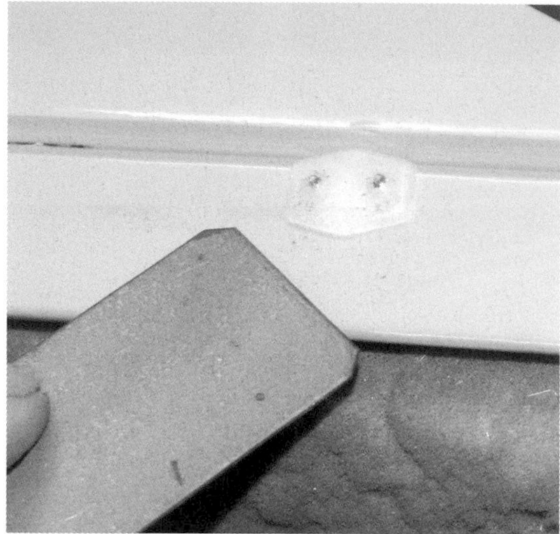

Projecting screws, on control horns, should be removed with a Permagrit tool, cutting and filing pianowire is best carried out with a Dremel tool.

any difficulties, but you may need a bit of help where they don't and any assistance in improving the model and its longevity should be worthwhile. One of the biggest dangers in assembling and fitting out an ARTF is to be in too much of a hurry, the very terms 'ready and almost ready to fly' seem to put an accent of speed on the project, but take your time, be thorough and the conclusion will be much more satisfying.

Tools

The instructions are likely to list the tools needed to complete the model, what they do not say is that they should be high quality tools. You will be fitting very small Phillips head style screws and unless you use a quality cross-head screwdriver the head will soon be chewed-up. Modelling, or craft knives must have sharp blades, quality blades will keep their edge longer and the type with a retractable blade, which can be broken away for a new section, are very useful as they can also be extended to give a longer cutting area. Heavy duty and needle nose pliers will have their uses, quality wire cutters will cope with pianowire of around 18g (1.2mm) but over that you will need a hacksaw, preferably fitted with a Permagrit blade. Permagrit tools are excellent for all shaping, cutting and 'sanding' jobs. It is often suggested that the wire ends of pushrods are bent with pliers, this is satisfactory for modest angle bends, but where a sharp right angle bend is required e.g. for inserting in a servo output arm and retained with a moulded nylon keeper, the only safe way is to insert the end in a metal working vice and bend it with a hardwood block. Unless the 90 degrees bend is sharp it will be impossible to fit the keeper, they can be a very tight fit anyway.

Drilling holes will be a requirement of most ARTF model kits and wherever possible these should be carried out with a vertical pillar drill to ensure that the holes are at 90 degrees to the component being drilled. This is of particular importance when drilling holes through thick tail surfaces or ailerons, to take the retaining screws for the control horns. The screws are passed through the horn, through the control surface and then into a moulding by self-tapping, if the spacing at the retention moulding is different to that of the horn it will not be possible to engage the screws. Incidentally, the screws supplied for retaining the horns are sometimes too short to project through

the aileron leading edge and these should be substituted for ones of adequate length, even if they are of slightly different diameters.

Universally disliked is the cutting of holes in GRP moulded engine cowlings to clear the engine, it involves a certain amount of trial and error work. You may be lucky and have in the kit a transparent cowling in addition to the GRP one, this can be used to mark out and cut the relevant openings before transferring the positions to the GRP cowling proper. Large irregular holes are best cut by drilling a series of small holes just inside the required cut line, adjoining one another, the piece of GRP can then be broken free and the edges smoothed with a file or a Permagrit tool. One of the quickest methods of cutting away the unwanted areas of GRP is by using a Dremel Moto-tool and a variety of discs and abrasive end pieces, this will save much time and frustration. It has been said that you can't have too many tools, but it is better to have fewer quality tools than a surplus of poor quality tools.

Adhesives

Mostly cyanoacrylates (cyano) and epoxy adhesives are specified for gluing components together, but other types are suitable. The important consideration is whether the adhesives and materials are compatible; polystyrene foams and cyano, with the exception of 'foam friendly' cyano, are not compatible, the cyano will eat away the foam. On the other hand some of the expanded foam materials, such as the Multiplex Elipor, are

Above, a 'part-picker' is indispensable for holding small screws and nuts etc. Permagrit tools will last a modelling lifetime. Right, A selection of clamps and pegs will be useful for holding components together while the adhesive dries.

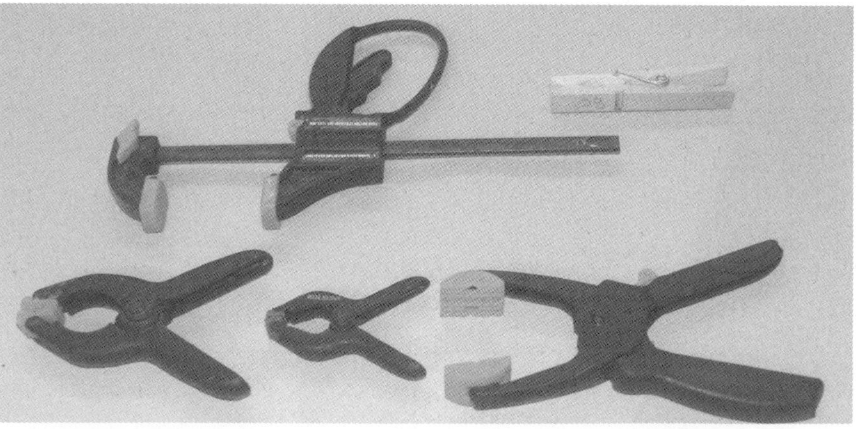

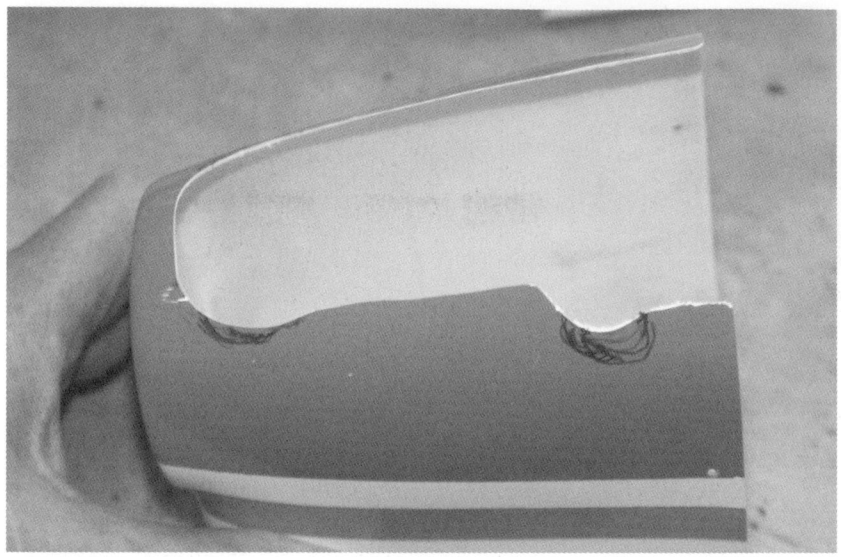

Cutting and fitting a GPP cowling is a matter of marking the area to be cut, using a drill, followed by a Dremel grinder to remove the unwanted moulding and trial fitting until a good fit is obtained.

best glued with cyano, the recommended method being to apply the adhesive to one surface and the activator to the other surface. The time that this method doesn't work is when a part is to be housed into a recess, the adhesive then 'grabs' before the part is fully inserted, use just the cyano adhesive for these occasions. There are a number of cyano types on the market, most common is the thin instant variety and this should be used with great care - once applied it may be impossible to move the joined parts, the slower drying, or gap-filling types may be a safer option. Instant, thin cyano is normally recommended for gluing thin vac-formed mouldings in place, the problem here is that the cyano is clear and it is all too easy to have it running down the covered, or painted surface. If this happens apply a cyano remover as soon as possible, using the ultra narrow tubing to apply the cyano in the first place will help to contain it to the areas of the joint, fit the tube into

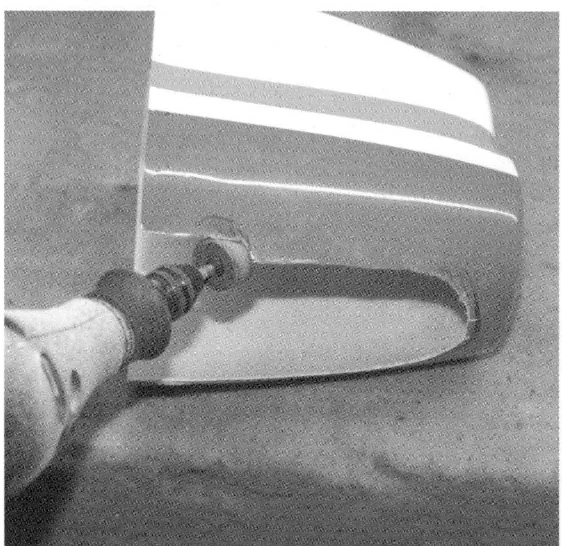

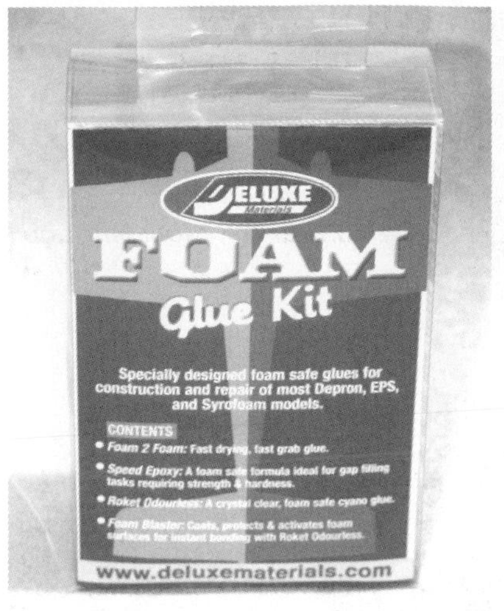

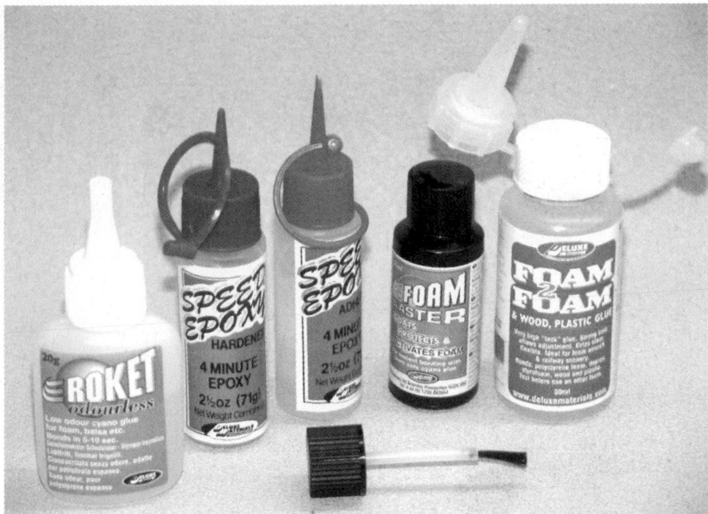

Adhesives for ARTF kits can be purchased individually, or as a Glue Kit containing the essential adhesives.

the bottle below the cyano, holding the tubing at the point of contact. Cyano can also be used for securing nuts to bolts, although a correct thread lock adhesive is better.

Two part epoxy adhesives come in gluing times from four minutes to 24 hours. Forget about the rapid glue types, they do not allow time to accurately position and secure before they start to set; also, if joining wood parts it does not give time for the epoxy to penetrate the fibres before setting. 20 minute is a good general purpose epoxy adhesive, possibly going to the one-hour type for high structural strength joints, such as joining wing panels. Epoxy adhesives set by chemical reaction and there is no loss of weight as the glue sets, so try to be reasonably sparing when applying it and wipe any excess from the joint with a rag soaked in meths (methylated spirits). For wood to wood joints the ordinary white PVA glue will also give a strong joint, providing the parts are a close fit, but remember that it will take longer to dry. It is essential to secure the parts to be glued together while they are drying, clamp if possible, or hold together with pins and masking tape.

Contact adhesives are not overly used with ARTF kits, for one thing the woodworking type will dissolve foam and the types used to veneer foam components do not have a part to play in most ARTF kits. There are many, many types of adhesives available for industrial and DIY users, they may be satisfactory for our models, but always test on scrap material first. Foaming adhesives may be considered for filling ABS vac-formed mouldings, such as lightweight pilots, dummy fuel tanks, floats etc., but beware, the two part action of foaming may continue for a long period and cause the mouldings to over fill and split the seams.

Whatever adhesives you intend to use the first cardinal rule is to check that the parts to be joined fit accurately. If they don't, cut, file and sand until they do - then apply the adhesive. Wing panels are usually joined with a wood or aluminium brace and it is important that this should be a free sliding fit into both panels, too tight and there will not be room for both the joiner and the epoxy

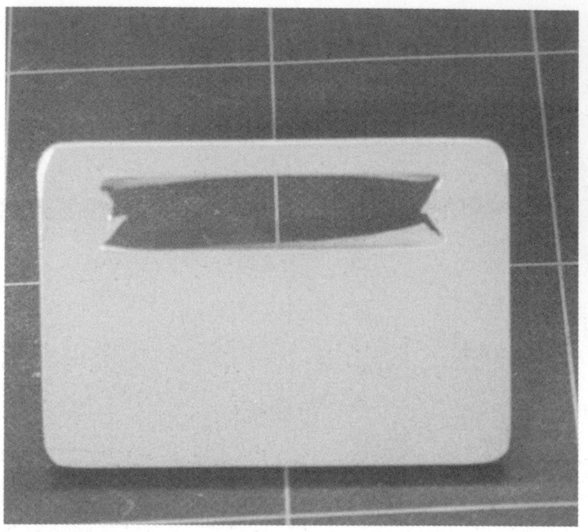

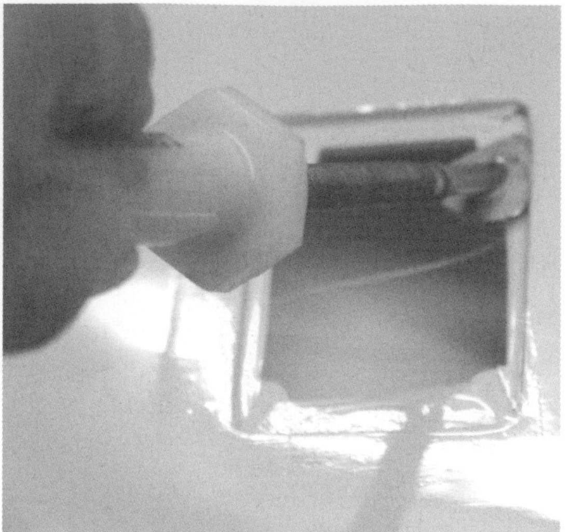

When openings are made in the film covering, the edges should be carefully ironed-down, small irons are available for these types of application.

adhesive. Also important is that the wing roots of the panel align, you can then clamp the panels together easily.

Built-up airframes

Balsa and plywood (sometimes including other species of wood also) airframes will be covered with film which may have gone a little slack due to different temperatures and humidity during transportation. Use an iron, a small travelling iron will do if you don't have one designed for modelling, to tauten the film where it is slack and also check to see whether there are any loose edges and iron these down. You may have to experiment with the iron temperature to find the correct setting; not all films require the same temperature. It will be necessary to cut openings for servos and in these cases don't cut to the full extent of the opening, cut about 1/8in (3mm) inside, cut diagonally into the corners and iron the edges down onto the thickness of the material. This will help to prevent the edges from picking up and the same treatment should be given to the slots for undercarriage wires and any other openings.

For IC powered models the engine bay will, hopefully, have been given a coat of fuelproof paint, but this will barely withstand the rigours of neat fuel spillage (especially if the fuel contains nitromethane) and exhaust gases. Give this area a generous coating of fuelproofer and at the same time brush proofer onto the wing seating area and down the inside of the fuselage at the wing seating, also the slot for the undercarriage and any other 'raw' edges of covering. You will have to cut away the covering film where the tailsurfaces are glued to the fuselage, if the edges of the film are covered by the joint there is no need to fuelproof, but it is always prudent to apply a run of proofer down the external joint in case there are any gaps. Any cutting away of film should be carefully undertaken, you are aiming to just cut through the film and not the wood beneath, if you think that you may inadvertently cut into the wood apply some cyano along the incision.

Undercarriages often prove to be the weakest part

of an ARTF model. There are a number of reasons for this, the most obvious being that it gets more of a hammering than other parts. You might be amazed how great a load is applied to the undercarriage, even in a reasonable landing, in a 'controlled crash' situation the stresses are enormous. Manufacturers do not always take these facts sufficiently into consideration and the wood blocks that take the top ends of the pianowire undercarriage legs may not be long enough or sufficiently well glued to the fuselage. Unfortunately it is not always possible to view these potential weak points and any work to strengthen the supports becomes remedial work after they have failed. Where aluminium alloy undercarriage legs are employed the metal has to have sufficient tensile strength to take the landing loads. A simple test is to hit the undercarriage with a metal rod, it should give a ringing tone, a dull sound usually indicates soft material. It is possible to strengthen undercarriages by adding a further piece of pianowire going from the axles up to the centre of the horizontal area located on the fuselage. This will help to prevent the legs from splaying out during a hard landing; the axle end can be retained by a soldered washer, the top with a nylon saddle.

Collets are the normal way of retaining the wheels, but these have a habit of coming loose and allowing the wheel to fall off. File a flat on the pianowire where the grub screw locates and apply thread lock to the screw. When manufacturers drill holes for the pianowire legs, at the fuselage, it is a simple straight hole, when they supply the legs the bends have a small radius and unless the corners of the holes are similarly radiuses the legs will not snug down into the slots. Cut and file the radius between the holes and the horizontal support so that the pianowire leg sits fully into the slot.

Wheel spats certainly add to the attractive appearance of a model but if you are to fly the model from a grass strip I would suggest that you do not fit them, they are too vulnerable and easily

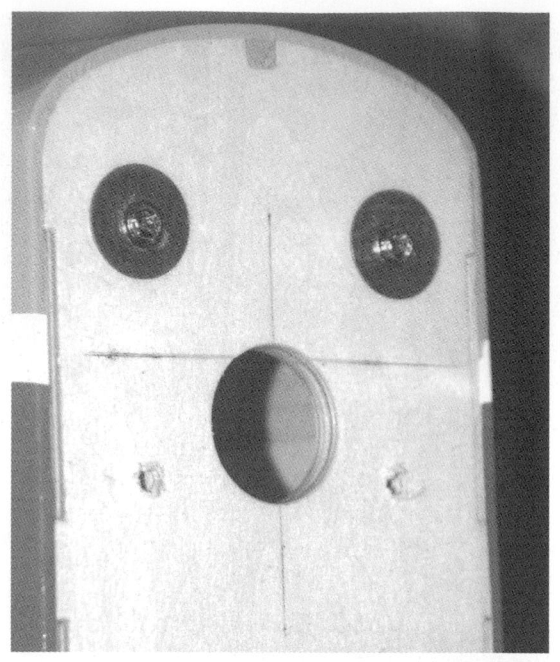

Engine Mounting

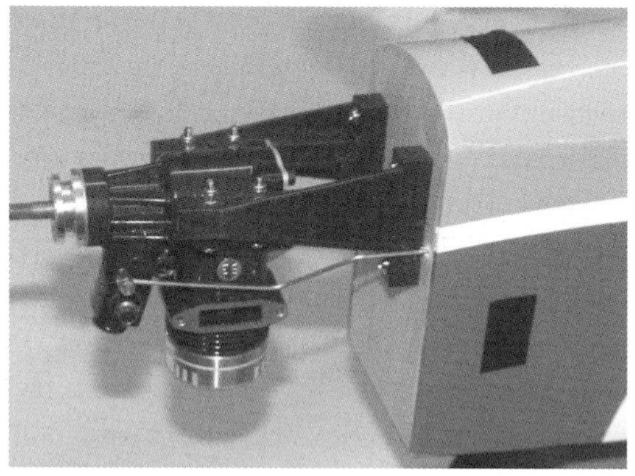

Engine mounting can take many forms but the principles remain the same. First, position the engine to give the correct measurement from the firewall (bulkhead) to the prop-driver. Mark the location of the bearer bolts and use the bolts to secure the captive nuts at the rear of the bulkhead, use large diameter washers when tightening and epoxy the nuts in position. With the engine fitted the cowling can be prepared for cutting and fitting, mark the location of the rear edges of the cowling with tape.

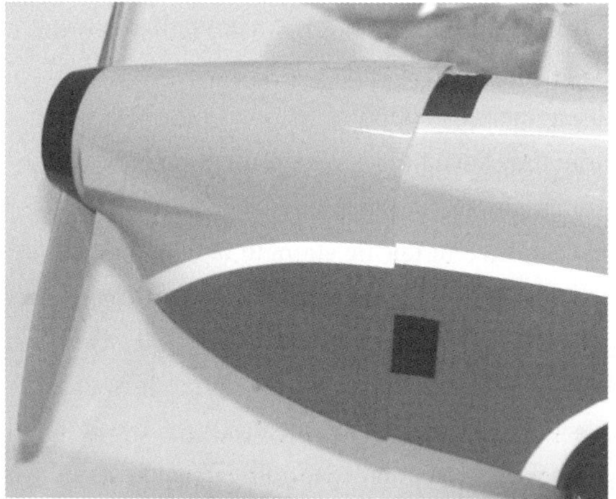

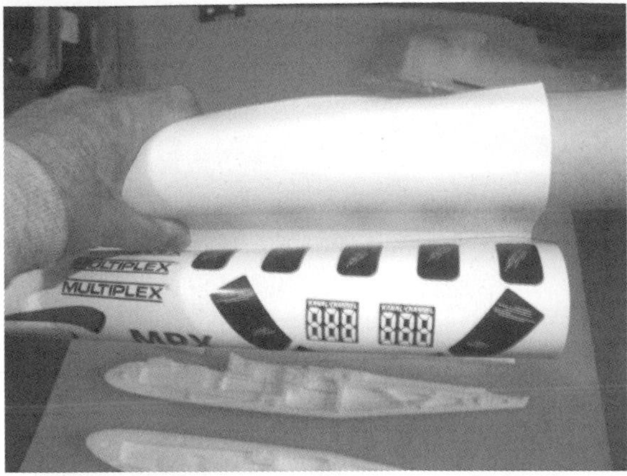

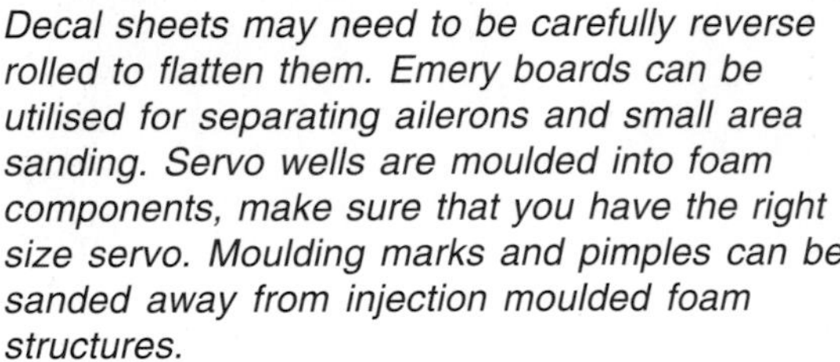

Decal sheets may need to be carefully reverse rolled to flatten them. Emery boards can be utilised for separating ailerons and small area sanding. Servo wells are moulded into foam components, make sure that you have the right size servo. Moulding marks and pimples can be sanded away from injection moulded foam structures.

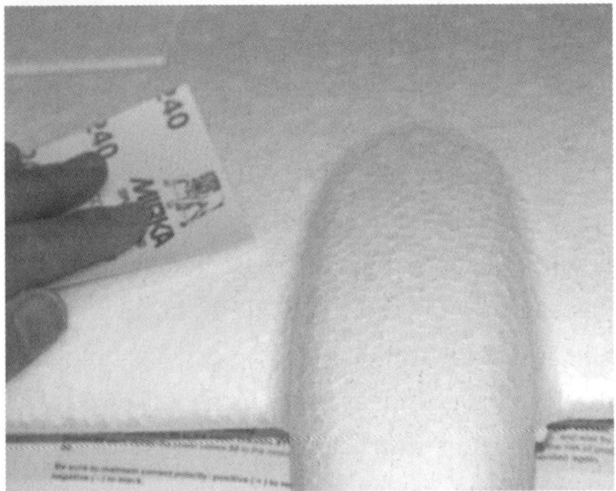

damaged. Leave the spats until you are a competent pilot and flying from hard standing or very short grass.

Engine installations can present problems, or to be more accurate, the engine cowlings covering the engines. When the model is designed there is an attempt to make it suitable for as wide a range of engine capacities and types as possible. The overall length of a '30' size two-stroke engine at one end of the scale and a '50' size four-stroke is considerably different, as is the mounting width, yet the engine mount and cowling has to cope with these variations. It would be stretching credulity to state that this is always the situation and that, without modification the smallest and largest engines of the specified range can be accommodated. A good reason for opting for an engine in the middle of the quoted range. For EP it is a different situation, either the motor is supplied, or the model is designed for specific motors.

Always check the stated dimensions for the prop-driver to the front bulkhead (firewall) it is not unknown for two different dimensions to be quoted, or for the larger capacity engines to be impossible to fit within the dimensions given. When it is ascertained that the engine will fit in the given length and to the width of the engine mounts, temporary mount the engine and mark the location of the engine bolts. Remove the mounts to drill the holes for the engine bolts. You should now have a positive dimension from the front

bulkhead to the prop-driver, tape the cowling to the fuselage so that the front of the cowling is approximately 3/32in (2mm) less than the prop-driver dimension, this can be ascertained by pushing a small rule through the front cowling hole. Mark the rear edges of the cowling onto the fuselage with a Chinagraph pencil, or non-permanent felt tip pen, and remove the cowling. Locate the positions for the cowl fixing screws and measure the distances from the marked lines, this will also give you the measurements for the holes to be drilled in the cowling for the fixing screws. If the holes for the screw come close to the cowling edge it is sensible to glue and screw further beech blocks to the front of the bulkhead for better security. Before the screw holes are finally drilled the engine must be positioned and the prop-driver centralised on the front of the cowling, then tape the cowling to the fuselage and drill small pilot holes, these can be opened up as necessary when the cowling is removed. This may all sound like a complicated method to achieve a simple end but it is important to follow the correct sequence.

Instruction Manuals often recommend that

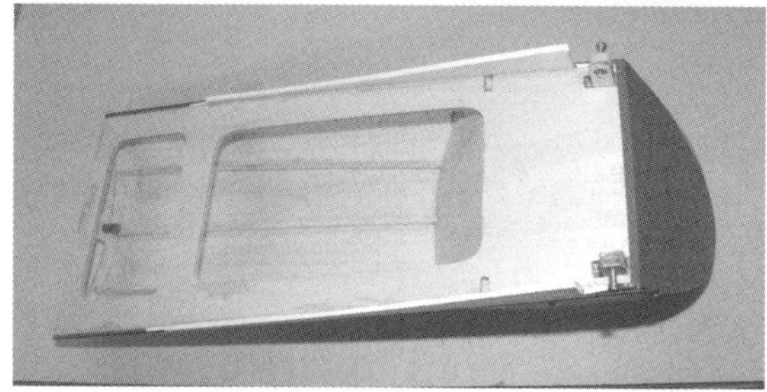

Never try to force a servo into a cutout, file the opening for a free fit. A 'Z' bender tool is useful for forming the 'Z' bend at the servo pushrod connection Positions for the radio equipment are often pre-located in ARTF models, note the foam packing under the receiver.

canopies be fixed with small self-tapping screws. This has the advantage of not risking getting cyano over the canopy or fuselage, but allows seepage of fuel between the canopy and the fuselage. Cyano should not be used for fixing canopies, as there is a real risk of the internal surface 'fogging' as the cyano sets. If you are not satisfied with just the screws holding the canopy, they may be locating into only 1/16in (1.5mm) balsa, use a combination of the screws and a proper canopy glue; the latter may take a day or two to dry where the canopy is glued onto film. Where the covering film is not pre-printed, decals are supplied to decorate the model; these are self-adhesive types where the backing sheet must be removed. Cut round the edges of the decal to be fixed before removing the backing sheet and be sure that you know where it is to be positioned. For small decals the positioning is relatively simple and if you do get it wrong it can usually be removed and repositioned. With larger areas of decals it is far more difficult to get the position absolutely correct - and fixed dry you only have one chance? For these larger decals it is safer to float them into position on a film of soapy water (a few drops of detergent in a bowl of water). When the decal is in the correct location dab it with tissues until the water is completely removed, work from the centre outwards to remove the water under the decal. It will take a day or two for the decal to be permanently fixed, but it will be in the correct position. If you have a string of letters e.g. aircraft registration, to affix, a piece of masking tape can be used to give the bottom line for the decals.

Fuel tanks

Suppliers of fuel tanks to the kit manufacturers seem to change from time to time, no doubt for economic reasons, so do check that the fuel tank fits in the space provided. If it is a twin pipe type and the model features a cowling; replace it with a three pipe tank. Where you are fitting an engine at the higher range of power the tank may be on the small size e.g. a 10oz (250cc) tank will not give a very long run for a '60' size engine and you may wish to fit a larger capacity tank, although this may involve some internal surgery to the fuselage. One of the annoying occurrences is when the holes in the fuel tank plates and bungs do not align, or the holes are not of sufficient diameter, or the bung is too large for the neck of the tank. Drilling and sanding can overcome all of these minor difficulties, but it need not happen with a little more care from the manufacturer, even in the low cost kits. Check that the metal tubing ends are free from burrs, it will help to fit the bung if some Vaseline (petroleum jelly) is smeared onto the bung before insertion. The silicone tubing used in the tank should not be too thick walled; otherwise it will not act as a 'clunk' tank. For fitting the front three silicone tubes through the hole in the front bulkhead the tubes should be held together with a small rubber band, thin skewers, or dowels fitted in the ends and these are then projected through the bulkhead. Either be generous with the silicone tube lengths and then trim to fit the nipples on the engine, or measure first. Where the front of the fuel tank fits the hole in the bulkhead any gaps can be sealed with bath silicone sealant.

Radio Installations

Recommended positions for the receiver and servos will be given in the manual, but it will often say to locate the battery to suit the balance of the model. That is fine if there is easy access to different locations, but that is rarely the case. For instance, once the fuel tank and engine/cowling have been installed it may need all of these items being removed to position the battery in a space above the fuel tank. As most of the ARTF models tend to finish tail heavy rather than nose heavy I would suggest a forward location for the battery as a first option. It may not be possible to fully wrap the battery in protective foam, but you can at least stick some 'Magic Foam' (self-adhesive foam strips about 3/16in. 5mm thick) to the internal

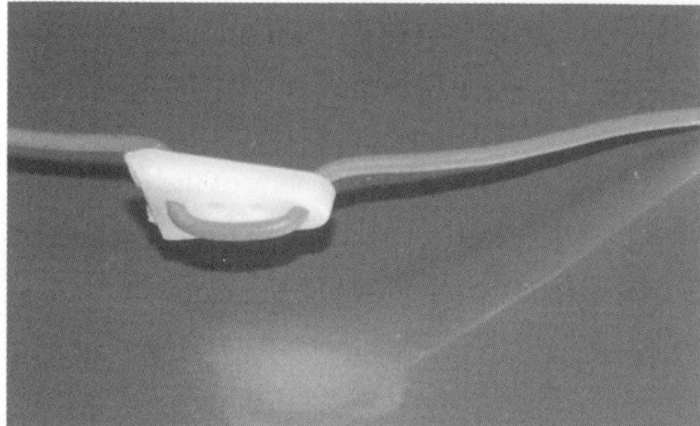

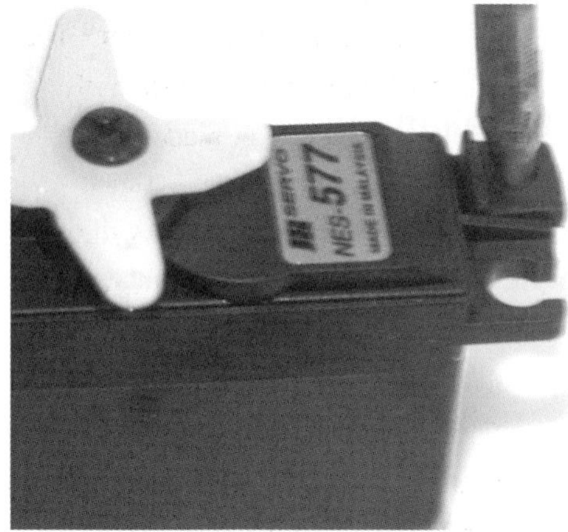

From the top. Use a piece of scrap servo arm to act as an aerial restrainer - it prevents the aerial from being accidentally pulled out of the fuselage. Servo lead extensions should have the plugs and sockets taped together for security. If you have to feed a servo lead through 'blind' holes in a wing, use a lead weight and cord to pull the lead through the holes. Servo grommets and the metal ferrules can be easily located using a dentists probe.

fuselage surfaces. Locate the switch on the fuselage side away from the silencer, or fit it internally with a switch extender, the switch should be close enough to the battery not to warrant an extension lead.

The receiver is a delicate instrument and needs to be protected from shocks and vibration; this can take the form of cocooning it in low and then high density foam or fixing it to the radio plate on resilient foam glued to the receiver base and the plate. The latter method is more suitable for lightweight receivers and the former for larger types - remember you may require access to the frequency crystal. Ideally the receiver aerial should be routed in a separate tube going from the radio bay to the stern post of the fuselage, the tube can be made from plastic drinking straws pushed together, the weight is negligible. Prevent any strain being put on the receiver to aerial joint by ensuring that the aerial is secured before it enters the tubing; a button, or clipped-off end of a servo arm, threaded through the aerial should act as a restraint.

Extension leads will probably be needed to reach

The most common form of control hinge is the furry Mylar hinge. It is glued (cyano) to the control surface and then, after checking alignment, to the airframe using 20min. epoxy.

individual aileron servos, try to use one of appropriate length so that there is not too much spare lead at the end. At the plug and socket joint it is prudent to wrap the joint with insulating tape, or use one of the proprietary accessories for retaining the joint. Where the lead has to be routed through a wing structure the manufacturer secures a length of thread at each end to act as a pull-through for the plug; when the servo has been located. Occasionally these leads will come loose, or you may drop one end and you have to fit a new length of line. This can be done by securing a small lead weight, a fishing line, or car wheel balancing weight to a piece of thread, hold the wing panel vertical and dangle the weight down the structure until it is visible at the servo location, the thread can then be pulled through the opening and secured. When a servo is removed remember to pull through a length of thread with it, so that you can fit a new servo lead. Servos are normally fitted to plywood plates, or hardwood bearers, with screws and rubber grommets but, for some installations, it is more practical to secure the servo using double-sided adhesive tape. In these instances ensure that the wood surface is well sealed, with clear cellulose dope or epoxy, before applying the tape. Separate aileron servos must have the output arm connections to give the appropriate control surface movement i.e. one up, one down and to achieve this the connections must either be both inboard, or both outboard of the servos.

Hinges

More and more the ARTF kits are coming with the hinges pre-fitted. This is a real time saver, but do check that they are truly secure, if the hinges are also pinned, so much the better; a good tug of the control surface will check the security. Give the control surfaces a good 'working' e.g. flexing, to remove any stiffness. For various reasons the hinges may not be pre-fitted and in these cases the most popular type of hinge supplied is the 'furry' Mylar version, often as a simple rectangle of material. They will probably be pushed into the pre-cut slots in the control surface, but not glued in position. Test the fitting of the hinges in the wing and tailsurfaces, this will be made easier if the corners are trimmed off the hinges. My favourite method of installing hinges is to use thin cyano for fixing them to the control surfaces, when it is easy to see where the adhesive is going, but do use 20 minute epoxy for gluing the hinges into the wing and tailsurfaces. I slip a piece of slotted polythene sheet over each hinge before applying the epoxy to the hinge surfaces, when pushed home this prevents the epoxy from getting onto the control surface. It is possible to use thin cyano to glue the hinge halves into the wing and tailsurfaces, by bending back the control surface and inserting the cyano, but I am never convinced that the cyano has filtered down to the ends of the hinges, so I then over compensate and finish up with cyano on the film surfaces. As before, check the security of the hinges by pulling on the control surfaces.

Linkages

Linkages between the servos and the control surfaces will take the form of a pushrod, or a tube within tubing, or a rod or cable within tubing. Occasionally a closed loop system will be used, with cables running from either side of the servo output arms to each side of the rudder horns. In each case a suitable form of attachment between the linkage and the servo output and control horn (or throttle arm) will be provided. It has to be admitted that the qualities of these fitting accessories does vary and these are the most likely items I replace. Clevises, whether plastic or metal, must be a snug fit on the control horns - also supplied by the manufacturer - and the

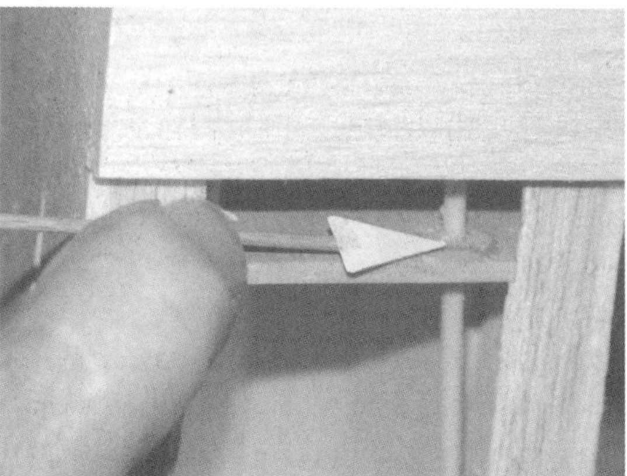

Plastic control tubes need to be secured to the wood airframe components in various places, either wrap the tube with masking tape and use epoxy, or apply Roket powder at the joint, followed by thin cyano adhesive. All forms of joints can be reinforced using Roket powder and cyano, the joint can be filed after the adhesive has set. Use the micro tubing in the cyano bottle, with the end into the liquid, so that the cyano can be accurately applied and the bottle kept upright.

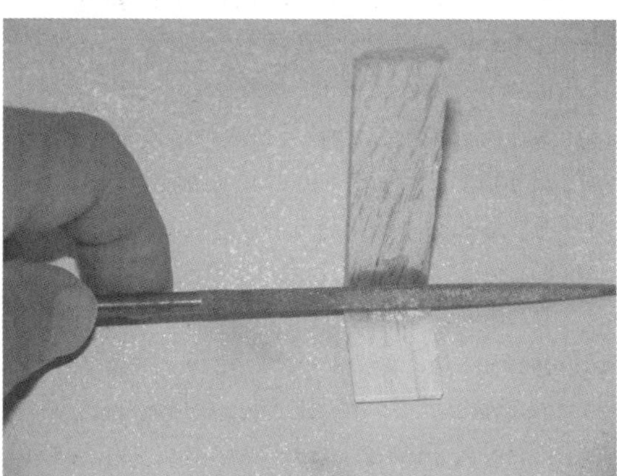

The all-important final check of the model is to ascertain the balance point. Low wing models can be installed on the simple balancer (previously described) by inverting the model, it should balance at the prescribed location in a slightly nose down (as on the glide) attitude.

clevises should be a good fit on the threaded ends of the pushrods, not too tight so that they cannot be adjusted, or too loose so that they can be pulled clear of the threaded rod. If you are at all doubtful of the suitability of these fittings, replace them, a failure could lead to a loss of your model. Sometimes the pushrod is fitted with a clevis at each end, this is satisfactory if they are fairly tight on the threaded rod, but if they rotate easily they could both turn due to vibration in flight and this would alter the length of the pushrod. My preference is for a clevis at the control surface end and a simple 90 degrees bend and good fitting keeper at the servo end, the bend must be made outside the fuselage to obtain a good, sharp bend - otherwise the keeper will not fit.

Where the servo tray is pre-fitted in the fuselage it would be helpful, where finished pushrods are not supplied, to give dimensions or, better still, a half scale drawing showing positions and angles of bends where they exit the fuselage. The forming of this 'dog-leg' bend on the elevator and/or rudder pushrods is difficult for the beginner to get right a it has to result in the correct alignment with the horns and be of the correct length between servo and the horn. One accessory, which makes the correct length of the pushrod less important is the servo connector, a device fitted to the servo, arm with a grub screw to secure the control rod at the required length. These simple connectors are good for small or medium sized models, but I would hesitate to use them in larger models where the loads on the servos are greater.

If control snakes (rods in tubes etc.) are being used instead of pushrods the outer tubes will probably be pre-installed in the fuselage, but they may not be secured. It is essential, to retain accurate control, that the two ends of the outer tubes, at least, are glued to the airframe. The plastic material may be of the "greasy feel" type which is not readily glued, either wrap the tubing first with masking tape before gluing, or use micro-balloons (or baking powder) around the tube to former location and then add thin cyano, this will hold it securely. You must, of course, be careful not to get any adhesive between the inner and outer tubes of the control snake; once glued they will not unglue.

Locations of control horns may be dimensioned in the manual, or may be obvious by the positions of the pushrods. Where these are the situations pre-drill the holes for fitting the control horn screws before the control surfaces are hinged or the tail surfaces fitted. It is so much easier to drill the holes accurately, on a pillar drill, while the control surfaces are separate than trying to achieve the same results with a hand drill and the fuselage and tail all in one piece.

With the radio equipment and linkages finally installed check that there is no binding of the hinges or linkages, it should all move smoothly with no obvious obstructions or catching - over the full range of movements. Equally, there should be no looseness in the linkages to allow lost movement, with the servo outputs locked in position it should not be possible to move the control surfaces in any direction; a small amount of movement, due to the flexing of the pushrod, is permissible, but any obvious free movement caused by excessively large holes in servo arms or horns, is not acceptable.

Final checks

The manual will denote the balance point for the model, also called the C of G (Centre of Gravity) although this term actually refers to the three dimensional centre of balance, use pieces of narrow adhesive tape to mark this location on the underside of the wing, for a high wing model and on the upper wing surface for a low wing model. If an acceptable range of balance points are quoted, opt for the forward location for the test flights, it will make for less responsive and easier to fly model. With the balance points marked, support the model on a balancing rig and adjust the battery location, or add self adhesive wheel balancing weights to the extremities until the lateral balance, with the model in a slightly nose down gliding attitude, is obtained.

A final check, too, that all the flying surfaces are correctly aligned on the fuselage and that there are no warps or twists in the surfaces. If you do come across a twist in a wing panel you can try heating the complete panel with a heat gun, twisting the wing in the opposite direction to the warp, holding it until it cools and, with a little luck, the twist will be corrected. The cure may not be permanent, so check from time to time that it has not reappeared.

All that is required now is a little patience to wait for some decent weather and a helping hand to give you your first taste of flying.

Repairs

It might be a little early to talk about repairs to the model, when you haven't even started to fly it, but it is best to be realistic. Most beginners to ARTF models will not have had an apprenticeship in building models from scratch and will not have an understanding of the constructional methods employed. I have heard many a traditionalist aeromodeller despairingly declaim, "Yes, he may be able to buy a model ready built and learn to fly it, but what is he going to do when he crashes it, he won't be able to repair it." There is a fair element of truth in this statement and the simple answer is that he won't try to repair the damage, he will go out and buy another model, or a replacement for the broken part. This attitude may seem shameful to the builder/flyer enthusiasts but if flying is the only final aim to the hobbyist it surely cannot be wrong to take advantage of the

Tears in the covering film can be repaired by applying PVA glue to the torn edges and then covering the whole area with Clingfilm; this helps to draw the edges together. After a couple of days remove the Clingfilm and apply thin cyano adhesive over the joints.

current situation of inexpensive imports. If we are golfers we are not expected to make our own golf clubs! The only reservation I would have to these attitudes is that the ARTF modeller will never get the full sense of satisfaction of the builder of the model who can admire his handiwork as well as his flying. Taking this argument to its limit, the person who designs his own model, builds it, engineers the engine and constructs the radio, will obtain the maximum satisfaction. I have only ever

The 'Micro Jet' is an agile model, electric powered with the propeller at the rear - and fast!

known one such gentleman.
Returning to repairs, I would suggest leaving these jobs to the knowledgeable, try to cultivate the friendship of an experienced modeller and learn from him. The only piece of advice I will give is in repairing tears in the film covering. I seem to be quite adept at dropping tools on the wing panels and causing a star shaped hole in the film. A trick I learned from my tissue and dope days and one that seems to work quite well with film covering, is to apply white PVA adhesive to the broken edges and then cover the whole area, generously, with Clingfilm - as used in the kitchen - and leave it for a few days. For some reason, which I don't pretend to understand, the edges are drawn together and the repair is effected, although it may be worthwhile reinforcing the joints with thick cyano adhesive.

Chapter 7

Learning to Fly

I have tried to emphasise the many advantages of joining a model club or flying group when learning to fly an R/C model aircraft. It is not only the actual assistance of teaching you the controlling of the model, but they will be able to check over the model to see whether you have made any unintentional errors. It is also a calming influence to have experienced modellers standing by to help if you get into trouble. There will be many questions you want to ask about the hobby, what happens if the engine stops, what if the model gets too high, or what do I do if it stalls? You can read books on the subject, I've written a few myself, but it can be more reassuring and immediate if there is someone at your shoulder to give a few words of comfort when things start to get tricky. Flying schools can give you the same assistance and reassurance; it is a pity that there aren't more of them scattered around the country.

A reminder here that if you are going to join a club, before you purchase your radio equipment take note of the make the club instructors use and the mode they fly and seriously consider purchasing compatible radios so that you can operate a 'buddy-box' system. This training method uses the instructor's master transmitter to which your transmitter is connected by an umbilical cord, when the instructor wants you to take command he simply presses a switch on the master transmitter and full, or partial control is passed to your transmitter. When you get into a difficult situation with the model, or he wants to demonstrate some aspect of flying to you, all he has to do is to release the switch and he resumes control again. Without any doubt this is the best way to learn to fly.

On your own

What if you can't join a club and don't have a

Although it is possible to learn to fly an R/C model aeroplane alone, it will be easier and less traumatic to obtain experienced assistance until you reach a proficient solo state.

training school near you? It leaves you with no option but to go it alone, after all, the instruction manual may well intimate that it is easy and that their training model will almost fly itself! Well, they would, wouldn't they! In fact, it is a narrow line between making the flying of an R/C model impossibly difficult, or ridiculously easy. For one thing it depends on the natural aptitude of the individual, some take to it with consummate ease, particularly the youngsters, grounded in computer games, and others find it quite a trial.

Lesson number one for the loner is that you should never be that - alone. It is vital to have someone to assist you at the flying site, to be a second pair of eyes and to launch the model for you; forget about anything you may have read

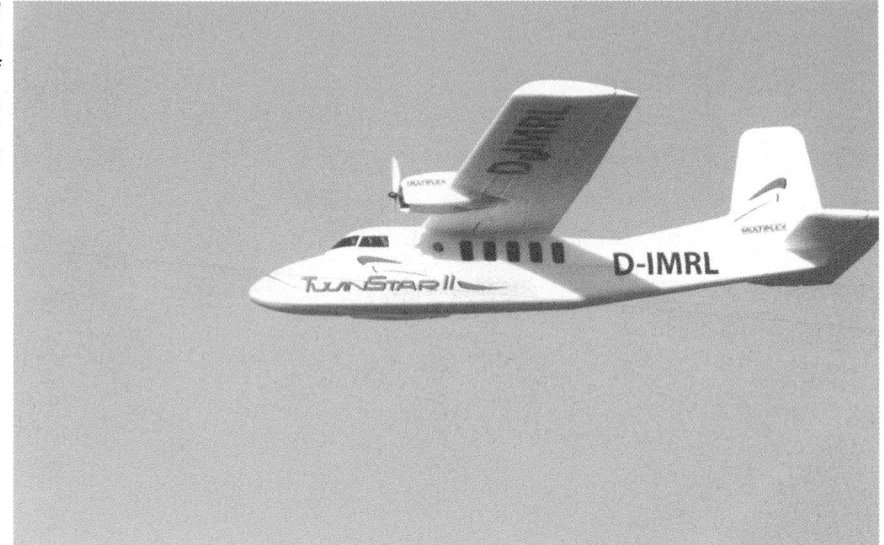

A twin engined model may not seem the obvious style of aeroplane for a beginner, but the Twin Star is a suitable candidate for this.

about launching the model yourself, you will have more than enough to do to keep the model going where you want it to, after launch, without anything else to worry about.

But, before we get to the exciting moment of the first launch there are a couple of suggestions, which could make learning to fly easier. Model flight simulators have improved enormously from the first basic types, with questionable graphics. I don't like the term 'Virtual Reality', nothing compares with the actual flying - and crashing of a model, but a simulator can take you a long way into the realms of R/C model flying. It gets you used to the attitudes and appearances of the model, it demonstrates the effects of control movements, the controls required when the model is flying towards you and all at no extra expense if you make a mistake. If you can afford, it purchase

Helicopters offer different flying challenges, electric power is a practical alternative to IC engines, allowing quieter and cleaner operation - and less smoke.

Many of the smaller (up to 40ins. wing span) will require hand launching try to obtain the services of an experienced aeromodeller for this operation.

a simulator where you can interface your own transmitter, this will get you used to operating all of the controls on the transmitter without having to look down to see where they are - not recommended when you are flying the actual model. It may be possible to obtain a simulator programme which features your actual training model, this is a definite advantage, forget about the exotic full-size aircraft simulations, they will not be of any help with your first faltering flights. Stability of the model i.e. to keep on a level keel is important and disturbing it from straight and level, into high-banked turns, or dives, is potentially dangerous. To assist you in keeping the model in level flight is a device known as HAL (Horizontal Aircraft Leveller). This has a light sensitive device, which is fitted to the underside of the fuselage that will automatically apply corrective aileron control, or rudder in the case of three channel models, in the case of unwanted banking of the model. Because of the additional weight of this system it is more suited to the '40' sized trainers and it should also be used in conjunction with a fail-safe system, the reason being that if the model did go out of range it could continue, thanks to the HAL system keeping the model level, flying for great distances with no guarantee of where it might land. With a fail-safe system all that is needed is for the transmitter signal to be lost to cut the engine/motor and for the model to descend.

Check, check, check

Before even contemplating flying the model you should ensure that the model and transmitter are fully charged and the airframe is checked for soundness. When you arrive at the flying site you should look around and try to visualise the area, the location of the trees and any other prominent features, when you are flying your eyes will be concentrated on the model and other features will only be in peripheral vision, it is important to be able to recognise them without having to take your eyes off the model.

Carry out a range check of the radio equipment, the manual should specify distances, with the aerial collapsed, for safe flying, carry out these checks both with the motor stopped and running, there shouldn't be any appreciable difference in

range with the motor running. When you have carried out these checks and familiarised yourself with the area, it is time to decide whether the wind conditions are acceptable for the vital first flights. The smaller the model the more critical are the wind conditions, for models under 40ins wing span, especially the small electric models, you should be looking for near to calm conditions, it may be frustrating to have to wait a day or two for that test flight, but you are more likely to have success in the right conditions. For the '40' sized trainer you can accept slightly stronger winds, providing they are of steady velocities and not gusty. You must also ensure that you have a clear flying area directly into wind and good landing approaches into wind; remember take-offs and landings must be directly into the prevailing wind.

Now, to attempt a take-off, or to rely on a hand launch? Two factors must be considered the model and the terrain. If you have very short grass on a smooth surface, or a tarmac or similar hard standing a take-off must be considered as the preferable option, if the model is equipped with a tricycle undercarriage and steerable nosewheel this further increases the desirability of a take-off. Another advantage of having these conditions is that you can practice controlling the model on the ground by opening the throttle so that the model is high speed taxiing, with a little down elevator trim applied to prevent any risk of a premature take-off, this will give you a feel of the rudder control and how to keep the model tracking into wind. Once you have mastered the ground handling go for a take-off, open up the throttle progressively, or increase the speed of the motor until the model lifts into the air, you may have to apply a little up elevator to achieve the lift-off, but be prepared to remove the up elevator once the model is in the air.

For tail-dragger models, ones with a tailwheel at the rear, and with rougher terrain on the flying site, a hand launch is the better option for getting airborne. Instruct your assistant to launch the model (with full power applied) directly into wind and with the model in a level, or slightly, nose-up attitude. Some instructions suggest a javelin like

When you are a proficient pilot you can try flying a P-51 Mustang - and giving an underhand launch, in the meantime stick with the easy to fly and launch models (right)

launch, but this is a little dangerous, the quality of the launch is important as much as the speed. Yes, the model must be launched firmly and it is easier to do this by running with the model to launch; the model is held at the balance point and pushed forward - more difficult to describe in words. The reason for launching firmly is simple, until the model reaches a flying speed i.e. above the stall speed, the controls are not effective, so running with the model before launching gets the model part way to that safety line, as does launching into wind.

The model is now airborne, from take-off or hand launch and we now have to control it until it is safely back on the ground. There are two schools of thought regarding the next actions, one is to fly

the model around to get used to the flying characteristics and controls before attempting to land, the other is to go straight into circuits and landings to give you the confidence of knowing that you can safely land the model at any time. Overall, providing that you are not a pessimist, I would suggest the familiarisation of the controls and flying before attempting the landing as the better option. Climb the model straight to a height of 100 to 150 feet (about the height of a church spire) and try a left-hand turn, after trimming the model for straight and level flight, by reducing the power setting. The greatest dangers of learning to control the model in these early stages is over controlling, giving too much aileron, or rudder control in one direction and then having to give excessive opposite control to compensate. Move the controls gently, if you have an exponential control adjustment on the transmitter set this at about 50% so that the control surface movement is less in the first stages of the control stick movements. Steering a model aeroplane is much the same as steering a car, you need to anticipate. With a car you don't wait until you have arrived at the corner before you turn the steering wheel, the same applies to a model aeroplane and don't wait until the model is well banked over in a turn before taking corrective action.

When I was learning to fly in the RAF my instructor would ask what happened when the aircraft was in a wrong attitude. My answer would be, "the aeroplane did so and so", "no", would be his reply, "the aeroplane didn't do that, you let it happen." Remember that you are, or should be, in control at all stages, the model will respond to your controls and you must make it go where you want it to go, not where it may meander.

Get the feel of the controls by turning the model in gentle left and right hand turns, maintain the height by increasing or decreasing the motor power, this is the control for ascending and descending, the elevator is for variations of speed (if you are not convinced of this fact just think about two channel models with only rudder and motor control, how could they otherwise ascend and descend). Orientation is one of the problem areas of learning to fly, knowing when the model is going away from you or coming towards you, the way to know is by never taking your eyes off the model and remembering the previous flight pattern. With the model coming towards you it can be confusing which direction to move the aileron or rudder stick when the model starts to bank. The old trick and probably the easiest to remember is to imagine you are propping-up the lower wing of the model with the transmitter stick to regain level flight. It is better to visualise yourself as being in the model to make the corrective actions, but this may only come with experience and any simple directive, such as propping-up the low wing, may prevent an accident.

Don't leave it too late in the first flight to practice your circuit and landing approach, you may need one or two attempts to get it right. Planning is the essential requirement of a good landing and that applied to any controlled aeroplane, model or full-size. The circuit should take the form of a rectangle whereby you take-off, climb to a safe height, carry out a 180 degrees turn to the left (or two 90 degrees turns with a crosswind straight between) continue on a reciprocal heading to the take-off and climb-out, followed by a further 180 degrees turn to bring you back in alignment with the take-off position. It is during the 180 degrees final turn that the power is adjusted so that the final approach to touch-down is carried out with as few adjustments to height, or direction, as possible are made. The secret of a good touch-down is in being set up on the approach accurately, the model will then almost land itself, only needing a touch of up elevator and final reduction of power to touch it safely down. If you are out of position on the final approach, offset from the runway, too high, too low, too fast or too slow always opt to overshoot and make another

From a high wing trainer the natural progression is to a low wing design, the Hana EP is easy to fly.

attempt; last minute dashes at the runway are rarely successful.

What are the most common errors in flying the landing circuit? Not going far enough upwind before starting your crosswind turn, the more so when there is a wind blowing. Flying the reciprocal downwind leg should be straightforward but there is often a tendency to 'crab-in' towards the take-off area and make the final turn too tight. Keep on a parallel course and then start the final crosswind turn as you pass yourself, how far you go downwind before executing the turn will depend on the wind strength, the stronger the wind the sooner your turn is initiated and the degree of bank and turn can be varied to allow the correct alignment with the touch-down point. Once in line with the runway adjust the distance (height) with the throttle stick and speed with elevator e.g. you may have to give some down elevator to keep the speed sufficiently high and some throttle to prevent the model losing too much height - it can be a juggling match! When you are a foot or two (300 – 500mm) above the landing area cut the throttle and give a little up elevator to round-out for a soft landing, not too much elevator or the model, if it is a little fast, may 'balloon' with its nose high. It is safer to land firmly than to stall the model into the ground.

How do you know whether a model is flying too fast or too slow? A difficult one, as models have different flying, therefore stalling speeds. What is a stall? It is when the model loses sufficient lift to keep flying and this will depend on the attitude of the model as well as the speed e.g. the model will stall at a higher speed when it is in a banked turn than when it is flying straight and level. The best way of learning about the safe speeds of your model and the response when it stalls is to take it to a safe height, close the throttle, ease back on the elevator stick and wait to see what happens. For most trainer models the stall will be fairly benign, the nose will drop and if the up elevator is then released the model will build up speed in the ensuing dive, then a small amount of up elevator, followed by an increase in power will bring the

Aerobatic trainers and sports models frequently feature a low wing design with tricycle undercarriage, it can hone your flying skills before attempting more advanced models.

model into straight and level flight again. One wing might drop as the model stalls; this can be picked up, when speed has increased again, by application of opposite rudder. Experiment with stalling the model in different attitudes, at different speeds and with varying amount of up elevator, providing you have sufficient height you will be able to recover and it will give you more confidence in your flying.

And what about the dreaded spin? Many high wing trainer models will not spin; they are too stable to be put into this autorotation mode. If, however you do get a model inadvertently into a spin, possibly through having a rearward balance point and excessive elevator and rudder movements, don't panic. Centralise the controls and the chances are that the model will recover into a straight dive of its own accord, if it continues to spin give some down elevator, to build up the speed and opposite rudder to the direction of the spin, releasing the rudder control as soon as it stops spinning. Gentle application of up elevator will then bring the model out of the dive and throttle can be applied to maintain height. The biggest danger in spinning is panic and freezing up on the controls, analyse what is happening in which direction the model is spinning and take the appropriate action. A spiral dive is often mistaken for a spin, but in this case the model is not stalled and will be in a faster diving turn. For recovery all that is needed is to give opposite bank control and up elevator.

It is a truism that you are not totally in control of an aircraft until you have put it into every conceivable attitude it is capable of attaining - and recovering from that position. Never fly a model aimlessly around, always have planned flying in mind and never stop practising approaches and landings. As some wit once said, 'take-offs are optional, landings are mandatory'.

I have not given any guidance on the suitability, or otherwise, of flying sites, this is because there are so many variables with regard to obstructions, approaches and surfaces. If you intend to fly from a non-established flying area it would be sensible to get some advice and to check whether it is legal

Before taking-off you should carry out the basic checks of control movements (in the correct directions?) and motor throttle control. Range checks need only be made at the beginning of the day's flying, but keep an eye on the state of the batteries.

to fly from it, many public areas do not permit model aircraft flying. Pick the largest obstacle free area you can find, if it is a field belonging to a farmer get permission to fly there and if it is grass see whether it would be possible to prepare a runway - although this is a luxury and looking to the future. Having a large landing area allows you to touch the model down over a fairly wide area, a boon when you are in the initial learning stages, but should not be an excuse for sloppy flying when you are more competent. You can often guess the flying site conditions of a modeller by the way he lands, one who has learned on a restricted site will nearly always land at his feet; it is all a matter of good discipline and training.

Last checks

After you have landed - or made an arrival - check the model over to ensure that nothing is damaged, the radio equipment has not moved, the propeller is sound and the wings and tailsurfaces are in their correct positions. When satisfied with this and made any corrections on the control linkages, so that the transmitter trims can be centralised and the model correctly trimmed (it may take a few flights to achieve the correct mechanical trimming) take a few moments off and analyse the flight you have just made. What went right and what went wrong and what parts you must practice again. Then you can fuel, or charge up for another flight. Learning to fly a R/C model is certainly the most rewarding time, but the truth is that we never stop learning. Every new model has different flight characteristics, every one offers new challenges and often they will spring a few surprises on the unwary. For the newcomer, more aerobatic than the first and then on to a fully aerobatic type to give you the opportunity to fly to the limits of your ability. From there on it is a matter of individual choice, there are enough ARTF models out there to satisfy the most diverse of tastes.

Chapter 8

More Advanced ARTF Models

For the initial stages of learning to fly the variety of training and sports models will keep you fully occupied, but there is a wider world of models to explore in the future. It is only possible to give a taste of the treats to come, as you become more experienced, read the R/C model aircraft magazines and attend rallies and shows you will naturally learn more about the avenues to explore, but here are a few of the possibilities.

Indoors

Indoor flying was once the province of rubber powered models, either the competition duration types, covered with microfilm and the stick and tissue models. Now, the ceiling - and walls - are the limit. In large halls, such as Olympia in London, I have seen IC powered models of considerable size and power, safely flown and even witnessed pylon racing with smaller models. The main limiting factor in these situations is the skill of the pilots. Over the years the R/C models have started to dominate and electric power has become the natural choice, due to its cleanliness, quietness and the increasing variety of motor and battery sizes. Radio equipment miniaturisation has had a profound effect on the design of indoor models and when it seems the limits of miniaturisation must have been reached, further developments take place, it would seem that the limits will be determined not by the electronic developments, but the size of our fingers. Certainly, living room flying is now a practical proposition and if the projects of the military are to be believed we will have to improve our eyesight to keep contact with forthcoming sub-micro designs. There is already a wide enough choice of indoor

Warbirds, such as the P-51 Mustang (previous page), and the 3D Tensor will improve your flying skills and add to the enjoyment and satisfaction - once you are past the learning stage.

electric R/C ARTF's to satisfy most modellers, they range from the 3D profile 'Foamies', or 'Shock' flyers, to sports and scale types and the increasingly popular small helicopters - small in stature, but fully blown when it comes to performance. Just when you think that it has all been done, along comes a company with a new concept, or a new twist on an old idea, what these introductions will be I don't know, but I am sure that they will come.

Outdoor

Outdoor scale ARTF models were once the laughing stock of the serious scale modeller, but no longer. There are some excellent renditions of scale aircraft in all sizes and they are becoming more accurate and convincing - and will continue to do so. Although the pre-printed film coverings are helping with the realism of models it is not easy for the manufacturers to include the nuances of weathering, but this gives the modeller an opportunity to add something of his skills to the finished project. All ARTF scale models can be improved in respect of authenticity, but many are now so good that the average modeller would be hard pushed to equal when conventionally building the same model. It is in the smaller and medium sized models that the scale designs really hit home. EP has allowed a vast range of moulded foam realistic scale designs to be developed, from pre-WW1 creations to the latest jet fighters - and they all fly! It must be borne in mind, however, that some scale models are more difficult to fly than others, don't expect to go straight from a high wing trainer to a scale ducted fan jet and cope, take your steps gently.

Aerobatics

Not so very long ago no self-respecting competition aerobatic pilot would have been seen dead with an ARTF model for his serious contest flying. How different now when you will hardly see a non-ARTF model in the arena, whether for pattern, 3D or Fun-Fly competitions. Some of the more serious competition contenders may only be produced in small batches, but they are still ARTF and there will be a minimum input by the competitor in respect of the airframe.

For public demonstrations there is nothing better than a large aerobatic model and these are available in ARTF kit form, usually powered by spark ignition, petrol engines.

Non-competition aerobatic ARTF's proliferate and offer excellent opportunities for flyers to improve their flying skills and explore the aerobatic repertoire.

Pylon Racers

A similar situation applies to the competition world of pylon racing, certainly in respect of serious FAI pylon racers. With these highly efficient, drag reducing airframes it is vital that they are produced in high quality moulds, completely free from flaws. It would be possible for a pylon racing contestant to make his own model plug, moulds and GRP moulded airframes, but it would be very time consuming and not economic. The same situation can be found with FAI class duration models, of sailplane, EP and IC types, the designs are now so exotic that professional building skills are virtually imperative and the competition more related to the flying and trimming skills.

Sailplanes

It is not only in competition classes that the skills of the GRP moulder are to be found, there are some superb, very large scale models of the highly efficient full-size sailplanes available. Expensive, yes, but absolutely magnificent and convincing in flight. More modest offerings are also on sale, both using traditional structural techniques as well as moulded foam construction of various types. If you are fortunate enough to live within easy reach of a good slope soaring site you've got it made, there are slope soarer models to be had in all shapes and sizes and at competitive prices. A popular type is the flying wing model, using foam structures these are nearly indestructible and could even be used as trainer models. For the less fortunate, where suitable hills are not available, or only on rare occasions, a compromise is to have the electric powered gliders. When natural lift is accessible it can be used, when not the motor switch is activated and the glider becomes a power model again. With a facility to switch off the motor in flight and for the propeller to fold back, we have returned the model to a glider.

Waterplanes

Flying off water adds another dimension to your flying, the satisfaction from executing a 'touch and go' on a glassy smooth lake cannot be over emphasised and the pleasure of take-offs and alighting makes any additional effort more than worthwhile. You obviously have to find a suitable site for these activities, but they are more numerous than you might first suppose, take a look at your local ordnance survey map and note the expanses of water indicated. There are some excellent ARTF waterplanes to be had, floatplanes and flying boats and separate float kits, which can be fitted to landplane designs. The downside of waterplane activities is that the models can, from a bad approach and touchdown, get very wet and traditional construction models, together with the radio equipment, must be carefully dried out before attempting to fly the model again. To this end, the all moulded model kits offer a distinct advantage, the water does not penetrate the structure and providing that the radio equipment is protected no harm will come to the model from a dunking; the engine can be emptied of water, the plug removed, a starter used to clear the last dregs of water and the engine re-started.

There are some unique designs around that are neither fish nor fowl, they start their operation on water, or land, looking like a cross between a

When you can hover a thousand pounds worth of model, vertically, a few feet off the ground, you know you have made the grade.

From pylon racers (right) to jet powered gliders, the range of ARTF kits is now almost limitless - and it is all waiting for you.

hydrofoil and a catamaran and then, as speed builds up these creations take to the air and perform like a conventional aeroplane. No doubt heli-boats, or some similar combinations, will be introduced before too long.

Large Scale Models

Large scale models, especially the 3D aerobatic types powered with large spark ignition engines are getting bigger and bigger and manufacturers are filling this desire for the 'bigger is better' modellers. There is no doubt that the larger the scale of the model the more realistic it is likely to appear in the air, but this development does not come without its risks. The larger, heavier and higher powered the model the greater the potential for damage and injury to persons. It would be grossly irresponsible to purchase a large ARTF model, weighing over 7kg, as your first or second

Most sports ARTF models can be modified to waterplane flying by the addition of floats - these are also available ARTF (Almost Ready to Float!)

model; safety comes with a gradual progression to the larger, faster and more aerobatic designs.

There is another very serious consideration when moving onto the giant models available in ARTF form. In the UK there is an upper limit of 20kg total weight - less fuel - of a model before it has to go through a very thorough design, construction and flying tests before it can be approved by the CAA for general flying. Some of the large imported ARTF models are getting very close and possibly exceeding this 20kg limit and would therefore be illegal in the UK. Remember, ignorance is no defence in law and to contravene the CAA regulations could result in heavy fines, worse still it would make any insurance null and void.

Gas Turbine powered jet models

Prior to the introduction of reliable commercial gas turbine engines, scale jet models were powered by

"Arrows-Smoke-Go". Emulating the Red Arrows Hawk, with smoke, is totally practical.

ducted fan engines i.e. a standard two-stroke glow engine fitted with a multi-bladed fan, operating in a duct. Although there were a few ARTF kits for semi-scale ducted fan power these have been largely superseded by those specifically designed for gas turbine engines (although the latest generation of electric motors and batteries promise ducted fan performances to equal those of gas turbines. First offerings have been scale kits for popular subjects such as the F-15 and F-18 fighters and the BAE Hawk fast jet trainer, no doubt that the range will increase to include other modern jet prototypes. Aimed at gas turbines with outputs from 12 to 35lbs thrust, this is very much a specialised area of the hobby and should only be contemplated by modellers with considerable

Large-scale models of light aircraft can be just as rewarding to fly as some of the 'heavier metal'.

Perhaps you would prefer an authentic replica of a 'Tucano' military trainer, powered by an IC or gas turbine engine.

experience of flying high-speed IC models. With speeds well in excess of 100mph and high 'G' manoeuvres there are calls for excellent piloting skills, spatial awareness and rapid reactions; the flight loads on the airframe are also very demanding and it is necessary to be able to inspect the ARTF airframe components and assure yourself that the quality of manufacture is adequate.

You can be assured that the designers and manufacturers of ARTF model aircraft will not only meet the future demands of the modellers, they will also be introducing new products, which haven't previously been tried. If you think that it's all been done, think again!

But, surely one of the dream replicas must be the 'Concorde' not available as an ARTF at the time of writing, in jet powered form, but who knows? It is the only way that you will be able to see this iconic aeroplane fly in the future.

Chapter 9
Aeromodelling Terms and Abbreviations

Glossary of Electronic Terms

General

ESC	Electronic Speed Controller
F/S	Fail-safe
R/C	Radio Control
Rx	Receiver
SMT	Surface Mounting Technology
Tx	Transmitter

Frequencies

MHz	Megahertz, as for transmission frequency, e.g. 35.020MHz
AM	Amplitude Modulation
FM	Frequency Modulation
IF	Intermediate Frequency
PPM	Pulse Position Modulation (same as FM)
PCM	Pulse Code Modulation
RF	Radiated Frequency
Syn or Synth	Synthesised frequency system
Xtal	Crystal (for frequency control)

Types

A or AIR	An R/C outfit suitable for aeroplane (power or glider) use
H or HE	For helicopter use

Channels/functions

4,5,6 etc.	Normally the number of channels or functions available
A, AIL or AILE	Aileron channel
Aux	Auxiliary channels
E, ELE or ELEV	Elevator channel
F or FLP	Flap channel
G, GER or GEAR	Undercarriage retract channel
T, THR or THRO	Throttle channel

Servo control setting

AST	Adjustable Servo Throw
ATV	Adjustable Travel Volume
D/R	Dual Rate
DSC	Direct Servo Control
EPA	End Point Adjustment
EXP	Exponential

Servos

kg/cm	Output torque of servo
LIN	Linear
NORM/REV	Normal or Reverse rotation of servo
Sec/60 degrees	Operating speed of servo
VTR	Variable Trace Ratio (soft centre)

Receiver

ABC&W	Anti-Blocking and Cross modulation and windows
DC	Dual Conversion
MPD	Micro Processor Decoder

Electrical

BATT	Battery
LED	Light Emitting Diode
LCD	Liquid Crystal Display
Li-Po	Lithium Polymer battery
mAh	Milli-Amp-Hour
MA	Milli-Amps current drain
Nicad	Nickel Cadmium battery
NiMH	Nickel Metal Hydride battery
V	Volts

Note:- Lithium Polymer batteries have different definitions to Nicads and NiMH, the cell voltage is 3.7volts and the battery pack will include a number of cells in series as a single unit, or two units in parallel. There will also be a 'C; rating notifying the maximum discharge rate e.g. 10C for a 500mAh battery is 5000mAh (5amp) safe discharge. An example of a Li-Po battery specification is 3s 2p 20c 800mAh i.e. 3 cells (11.1v) with two batteries in parallel, a maximum discharge rate of 16 amps and a capacity of 800mAh.

Transmitter layouts are referred to as Mode 1 or Mode 2. Mode 1 has the aileron and throttle controls on the right hand stick and the elevator and rudder controls on the left hand stick. Mode 2 features the aileron and elevator controls on the right hand stick and the throttle and rudder on the left hand stick.

Glossary of Aeromodelling Terms

Aerobatics	Advanced manoeuvres performed by an aircraft.
Aliphatic resin	Water-based adhesive that dries crisply and is used for basic wood joints.
Amphibian	Aeroplane capable of operating from both land and water.
ARF & ARTF	Almost ready to fly model, supplied in kit form for quick assembly.
ARTC	Almost ready to cover kit.
Autogyro	Aircraft with freely rotating rotors and conventional engine and propeller thrust.
Balloons	Lightweight filler in the form of micro glass spheres; it is mixed with epoxy.
Bellcrank	Used for changing direction of linkage through 90 degrees by means of a pivoting plate.
Biplane	Aeroplane having two wings, one above the other; when the lower wing is less than 50% area of the top wing it is known as a sesquiplane.
Blind nut (Anchor nut)	Secured nut which, when fixed to wood, will allow a bolt to be screwed in and out without need to access the nut.
Bulkhead	Front fuselage former, also known as the firewall.
Carbon fibre	Extra strong material used for reinforcing structures and nylon mouldings.
Centre section	Centre area of wing adjacent to fuselage, usually flat.
Chamfer	Angled cut on material.
Charger	Electronic unit for charging cells, e.g. nickel cadmium, nickel metal hydride and 'wet' and 'gel' cells.
Clevis (Snap link)	For connecting pushrods to control horns and servo arms and to give adjustment of length. Also available in ball link form with ball and socket joint.
Closed-loop control	Pair of cables connected to each side of the servo output and control horns to act in a pull-pull movement of the control surface.
Clunk tank	Fuel tank with weighted fuel pick-up on a flexible tube for filling in all aircraft positions.
CNC	Computer numerically controlled machine parts are very accurate and repeatable.
Collet	For retaining wheels to undercarriage legs.
Compression ignition engine	More commonly known as the diesel engine.
Cowling	Enclosure around the engine, normally removable.

Cyanoacrylate	Rapidly acting adhesive, also known as instant and miracle glue. Available in various viscosities.
Dope	Generic name for nitrate and buytrate cellulose finishes. Shrinking dope is used for tautening tissue, silk and nylon, non-tautening dope for filling the weave.
Doubler	Second layer of balsa or plywood to reinforce a structural area.
Dremel	Manufactured series of motorised tools.
Dural	Aluminium alloy used for undercarriages, etc.
EP	Electric power
Epoxy	Two-part adhesive with setting times from four minutes to twenty-four hours. Good for wood, metal and plastics.
EPS	Expanded polystyrene. Available in various densities and used for veneered wing cores, etc.
Firewall	Front bulkhead to which the engine bearers or mount are fitted.
Flight box	Portable box containing all the tools, accessories, fuel and starting equipment required at the flying site.
Floats	For flying models off water and replacing the normal undercarriage and wheels.
Flying boat	Aeroplane utilising a boat-type hull to allow the taking off and alighting on water.
Flying wing	Aeroplane with no tail surfaces.
Glass fibre (GPR)	Glass woven cloth or mat, layered with epoxy resin to form mouldings or skinning of veneers.
Glider	Unpowered aircraft.
Glow engine	Internal combustion engine using a glow plug for igniting the fuel/air mixture.
Glow plug	Platinum wire coil in the ignition plug is initially heated with a battery, but continues to glow, when the engine is running, by compression.
Heat-shrink covering	Commercially available plastic film and fabric covering materials in a wide range of colours. Applied with a hot iron to activate the adhesive, they are tautened by a furthcr application of heat.
Helicopter	Aircraft deriving lift from powered rotors.
Horn	Control horn for fitting to elevators, rudder and ailerons to which the pushrod linkage is connected.
IC	Internal combustion, i.e. glow, diesel and spark ignition engine.
Jet	Gas turbine engine or an aircraft powered by a gas turbine engine.
Jig	A building aid to hold components in place during construction.
Keeper	Moulded accessory for retaining wire pushrod ends to control horns and servos.
Laminate	Multi-layers of material glued together to give increased strength, as in laminated tail-surface outlines.
Landing gear	Alternative name for undercarriage.
Linkage	Mechanical connection between the servos and control surfaces and other controls.

Liteply	Lightweight form of plywood.
Longeron	Longitudinal spars in the fuselage.
Mylar	Plastic material used to form control-surface hinges.
Ornithopter	Aircraft creating flight by flapping its wings, as with a bird.
Permagrit	Commercial range of abrasive tools.
Piano wire, music wire	High-tensile steel wire used to form undercarriages, etc.
Planform	Aircraft viewed from directly above.
Planking	Sheeted areas formed with narrow strips of wood.
Polyhedral	Wing, or other flying surface, having three or more dihedral breaks.
Polypropylene	Flexible plastic used for moulded control-surface hinges.
Prototype	Original design, which can be used to describe the full-sized aircraft from which the model is based.
PTFE tube	Polyterafluoroethylene, a lightweight smooth-walled plastic tubing used for control linkages.
Pusher	Aeroplane with the engine located in front of the propeller.
Pushrod	Linkage between the servo and the control horn, normally in rigid form.
PVA (Polyvinyl acetate)	White glue, moderately slow drying, suitable for wood to wood joints. Also available in 'waterproof' quality.
PVC (Polyvinyl chloride)	Clear plastic sheet used for moulding cockpit canopies, etc.
Razor plane	Miniature wood plane using a razor blade as the cutting element.
Razor saw	Very fine-toothed small saw for cutting thicker balsa strip and sheet.
Receiver (Rx)	Electronic unit located in the aircraft for receiving signals from the transmitter.
Retracts	Retractable undercarriage mechanism.
Root	Innermost rib of a lifting surface to the fuselage or centre.
Safety nut	Domed propeller retaining nut, rounded for safety reasons.
Scale model	Miniature flying replica of a full-size aircraft.
Seaplane	Model capable of taking off and landing from water.
Servo	Electro-mechanical actuator taking the signals from the receiver and translating them into movements of the control linkages.
Sheeting	Thin balsawood, or other woods, covering an open framework.
Side view	The aircraft viewed exactly from the side.
Silicone	Tubing used for connecting the fuel tank and the engine and in semi-liquid form as a filler and water-proofing sealant.
Slope soarer	Glider relying on obtaining lift through the air rising from sloping ground.
Snake	Common name used for a control linkage constructed from a flexible rod, or small tube, inside a larger diameter outer tube. Where stranded steel cable is used for the inner it is known as a Bowden cable.
Spar	Spanwise structural member to which the wing ribs are attached.

Sweep back — Angle of the wings, rearward, relative to the lateral datum.

Tailless — Aeroplane without any tail surfaces.

Tailplane — Fixed portion of the horizontal tail surface to which the elevators are hinged.

Template — Metal or wood pattern used to form similar parts in a variety of materials.

Test stand — Instrument for holding a model engine firm and when test running.

Thermal soarers — Gliders reliant on warm air currents to stay in the air.

Torque rod — Rod, supported in a tube, which imparts movement from one end to the opposite end.

Tractor — Propeller in front of the engine, pulling the aeroplane.

Transmitter (Tx) — Hand-held radio-control emitter of radio signals to the receiver.

Trim — Minor control movements operated by adjustments of the trim controls on the transmitter, adjacent to the main control sticks.

Triplane — Aeroplane with three wings.

V-tail — Tail surface configuration where the rudder and elevator controls are operated in the diagonal 'V' formation.

Wing ribs — Aerofoil section components to support the wing covering.

3D — Name given to models capable of performing extreme manoeuvres.

Glossary of Aerodynamic Terms

Aerofoil (Airfoil) — Cross section of a lifting surface such as an aircraft wing.

Aileron — Movable control surface on the wing to control roll.

Angle of attack — Angle at which a lifting body is presented to the air in flight.

Angle of incidence — Angle of the wing and other surfaces relative to a datum line shown on the plan drawings.

Aspect ratio — Ratio of the span to the area.

Balance point — Point at which the model will balance, normally in the horizontal plane.

Ballast — Weight added to a model to adjust the balance point, or increase the wing loading.

Bank — Lateral angle of the model in a turn.

Centre of gravity (C of G) — Point at which the model will balance in both the horizontal and vertical planes. Often incorrectly used for the horizontal balance point only.

Centre of pressure — Point on the wing at which the centre of lift acts.

Chord — Width of the aerofoil.

Control surface — Movable area of the aerofoil to vary the lift and cause a change of direction.

Datum line — Construction reference line from which all measurements and angles are made.

Dihedral — Upward angle, towards the tips, of a lifting surface.

Down thrust — Downward angle of the thrust line (motor) relative to the datum.

Drag — Combined resistance of the airframe to movement through the air.

Elevator	Control surface, attached to the tailplane, to control pitch movements.
Elevons	Combined elevator and aileron functions, as used on canards and deltas.
Fin	Fixed portion of the vertical stabilising surface.
Flaperons	Combined flap and aileron functions.
'G' forces	Increased load on the aircraft due to centrifugal forces (as in looping manoeuvres).
Lift	Force acting at right angles to the flight direction, overcoming gravity.
Pitch	Rise and fall of the aircraft nose relative to the line of travel. Also a term to describe the theoretical distance travelled by the tip of a propeller in one revolution.
Roll	Movement of the aircraft around the longitudinal axis.
Rudder	Movable control surface attached to the fin.
Span	Dimension from tip to tip of a lifting surface.
Stability	Ability of the aircraft to stabilise to a flight attitude as dictated by the control inputs.
Stall	Loss of lift resulting from an excessive angle of attack.
Thrust	Force provided by the propeller, jet or rocket, or as a function of gravity.
Torque effect	Reactive force produced by a rotating propeller, normally counteracted by the use of engine side thrust or rudder offset.
Upthrust	Upward angle of the engine propeller shaft respective to the model datum.
Wash-in	Downward twist in the wing trailing edge towards the tip.
Wash-out	Upward twist in the wing trailing edge towards the tip.
Wing loading	Relationship of the wing area to the total weight of the aircraft.
Yaw	Rotation of the aircraft around the vertical, initiated by the movement of the rudder.

Chapter 10

Useful Contacts

GOVERNING BODY

The governing body of aeromodelling in the UK is the British Model Flying Association (BMFA), which is responsible for the general regulation of the sport and the FAI records and competitions. Most clubs are affiliated to the BMFA and membership includes insurance and a quarterly publication, The BMFA News. The address for the BMFA is:

British Model Flying Association
Chacksfield House
31 St Andrews Road
Leicester
LE2 8RE
Tel: 0116 2440028 Fax: 0116 2440645
Website: www.bmfa.org
E-mail: admin@bmfa.org

The BMFA also recognise Specialist Bodies, e.g. Electric Flight, Helicopters, Aerobatics etc., details can be obtained from the BMFA, and also the contacts for affiliated clubs in your area.

CIVIL AVIATION AUTHORITY

Civil Aviation Authority
Aviation House
Gatwick Airport
Southwest Sussex
RH6 0YR
Tel: 01293 567171

The CAA, under the Air Navigation Order 1955 regulates all flying in the UK, be it full-size or models, and makes regulations governing model flying.

LARGE MODEL ASSOCIATION

Chris Bland, Secretary
Ringwood,
Ashton Road
Lancaster
LA2 0AA
Tel. 01524 63609
Website: http://www.LargeModelAssociation.com

MANUFACTURERS AND DISTRIBUTORS

Amerang

Lancing Business Park
Commercial Way
Lancing, West Sussex
BN15 8TA
Tel: 01903 765496

Belair Model Supply Co.

Unit 7, Royson Way
Dereham Business Park
Dereham, Norfolk
NR19 1WD
Tel: 0845 2606677

Century UK Ltd.

7 Anchor Business Park
Castle Road
Sittingbourne, Kent
ME10 3AE
Tel: 01795 437056

CML Distribution Saxon House
Saxon Business Park, Hanbury Road
Bromsgrove, Worcs.
B60 4AD

Flight Power UK Tel: 01279 777111

Helgar Distribution

2/4 Playters Road
Staple Tye, Southern Way
Harlow, Essex
CM18 7NS
Tel: 01279 641097

J Perkins Distribution Ltd.

Northdown Business Park
Ashford Road
Lenham. Kent
ME17 2DL
Tel: 01622 854300

Just Engines Ltd.

Newby Cross Farm
Newby Cross, Carlisle
CA5 6JP
Tel: 01228 712800

MacGregor Industries Ltd.

Cordwallis Street
Maidenhead
SL6 7GF
Tel: 01628 760431

Motors & Rotors

Unit 2, 13 Smith Street
Watford, Herts.
WD18 0WE
Tel: 01923 465712

Multiplex Modellsport GmbH & Co. KG

Neuer Weg 2
D-75223 Niefern
Germany
UK Contact Gordon Upton Tel: 0792 1166645

)vertec

Unit 1, Jesmond Dene Trading Estate
School Lane, Forton
Nr. Lancaster, Lancs.
PR3 0AT
Tel: 01524 793328

Puffin Models

Unit D3 Backfield Farm
Wotton Road
Iron Acton, Bristol
BS37 9XD
Tel: 01454 228184

Ripmax Ltd/Irvine

241 Green Street
Enfield
EN3 7SJ

Sola Models 4 Church Street
Uckfield
East Sussex
TN22 1BJ
Tel: 01825 760847

Steve Webb
80 Church Street
Frodsham, Cheshire
WA6 6QU
Tel: 01928 735225

Snelflight
Unit 6, Portsmouth Enterprise Centre
Quartermaine Road
Portsmouth
PO3 5QT
Tel: 022392 69966

Sussex Model Centre
57-59 Broadwater Road
Worthing
West Sussex
BN14 8AH
Tel: 01903 207525

Weston UK
84-88 London Road
Teynham
Sittingbourne, Kent
ME9 9QH
Tel: 01795 521030

TRAINING SCHOOLS

Aerial Training Services
Hangar One, Draycott Farm Aerodrome
Chiseldon, Swindon, Wilts
SN4 0HX
Tel: 01793 740666

Go Solo
1 Manor Farm Lane
Oldbury, Bridgenorth
Shropshire
WV16 5HG
Tel: 01746 762563

Midland Flight Training School
Tel: 07711 963939

Paul Heckles School of Flying
Tel: 07866 599988

Scallywags Models Tel: 0121 2505520

MODEL MAGAZINES

R/C Model Flyer and Rotor world
ADH Publishing
Doolittle Mill, Doolittle Lane
Totternhoe, Beds.
LU6 1QX
Tel: 01525 222573

Radio Control Models & Electronics (RCM&E)
Magicalia Ltd
Berwick House, 8-10 Knoll Rise
Orpington, Kent
BR6 0EL
Tel: 01689 899200

R/C Model World, Jet International and Quiet & Electric Flight
Traplet Publications Ltd
FREEPOST WR553
Worcester
WR8 9BR
Tel: 01684 575979

Chapter 11

ARTF Reviews

Flying R/C Toys

When does a toy become a model'? There is no obvious distinction between moulded foam remote control toys, as found in toyshops and emporiums such as Woolworths. Argos and Comet and similar products sold in hobby and model retailers. Perhaps the 'models' tend to be slightly more sophisticated and expensive, but whether they are referred to as toys or models is

immaterial, they are performing the same *function*. Typical of smallest and least expensive of these R/C aeroplanes are the twin electric motor, all foam designs with wingspans of only 10 to 12 (250 – 300mm) inches and costing around £30. Why the complication of twin motors? By varying the individual speeds of the motors it is possible to directionally control the model and by increasing

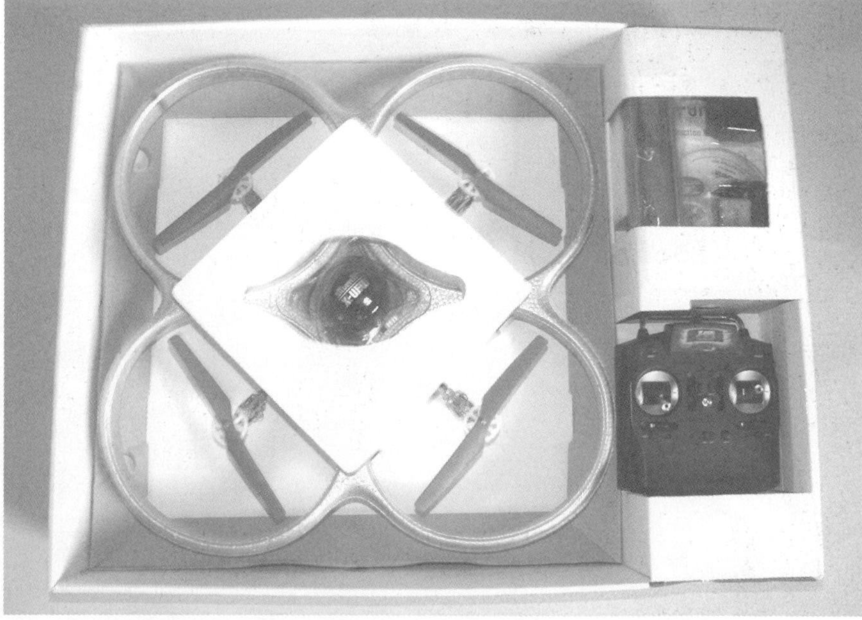

or decreasing the power to both engines ascent or descent is possible, all without the need for electronic actuators and control surface movements. Attractively packaged these toys come complete, no work to do on the aeroplane, they are ready for flying, the two function transmitter is on 27mHz band and charging of the small Lithium battery in the plane is usually via the transmitter. The only extras needed, before flying, are dry pen cell batteries for the transmitter, a quick charge and you are ready to test your flying skills.

Slightly more sophisticated and expensive offerings may feature separate rudder controls, though not necessarily proportional control and separate mains or 12 volt chargers. From there on the degree of control of the aeroplane is improved by the addition of elevator function and eventually to a 'full house' control of motor, ailerons, elevator and rudder and then we are certainly in the realms of models.

There is such diversity of these ingenious little all foam, genuinely ready to fly R/C aeroplanes that it

is impossible to review them individually, but at the low costs there is not too much at stake and if given, or received as presents it should he possible to experiment with different types. The examples with proportional control, rather than fully on or off rudder and elevator control of some of the earlier toys, are easier to operate.

Watch out for

The biggest limitation with these mini-models is undoubtedly their inability to cope with windy conditions. As they are primarily aimed at the younger generation this may be a hard lesson to learn, patience is not one or the strongest virtues of the young and they will want to go flying in less than ideal conditions, it will end in disappointment.

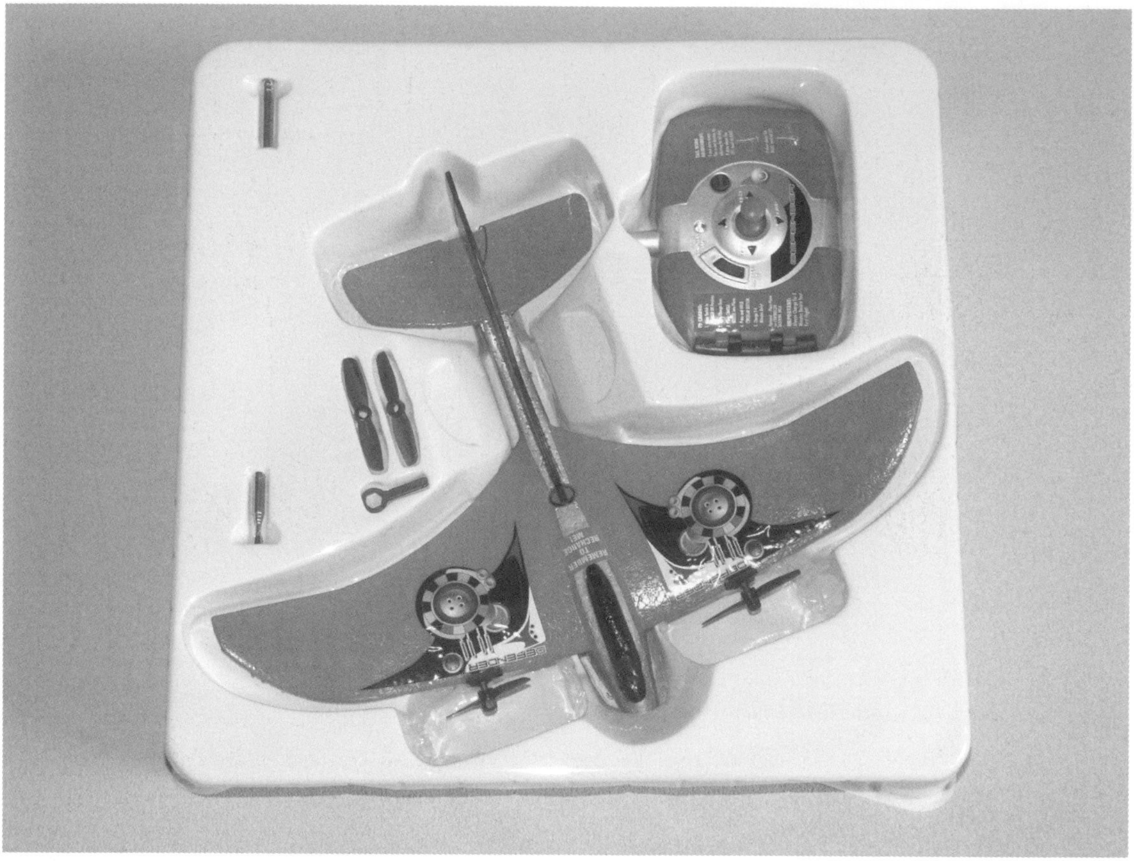

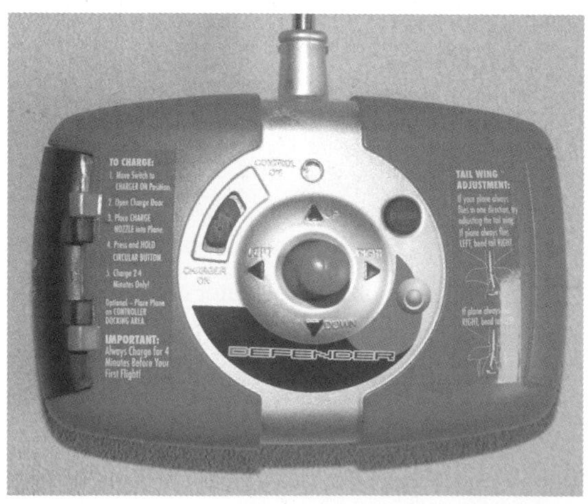

With the only additional purchase being the dry batteries for the transmitter do not skimp on these, buy long-life types and these will last longer when these batteries are also the source for charging the airborne battery. Standards of English in the instructions can be variable with such comments as “pack the battery with the right direction to refresh”, when they actually mean, ensure that the plug is correctly inserted when the battery is to be charged. Distributors addendum notes may be included, if not, try to interpret the meaning, it is unlikely that you will do any major damage.

Flight qualities

Although the models are small they are not highly manoeuvrable and you will need a good

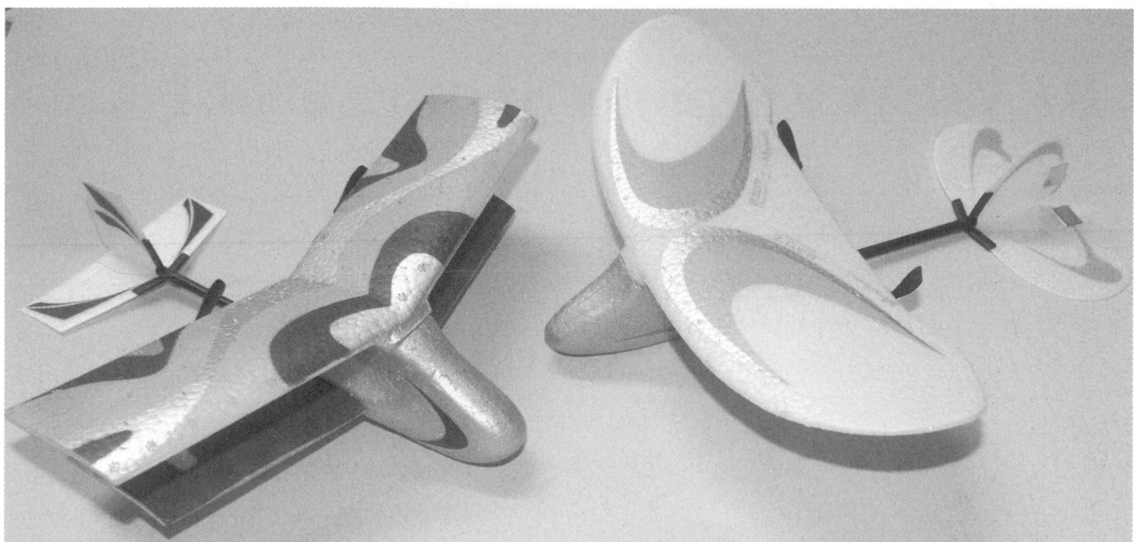

open area in which to fly them. If they are classed as toys it should be possible to fly them in parks and recreation grounds, they are light and are not potentially dangerous - certainly when compared with a cricket ball - and the pushers are particularly safe. Because the variable speed control on each motor is less responsive than rudder and elevator controls it is important to anticipate changes of direction, otherwise you will be constantly trying to recover from awkward positions. Flying them in even a light wind is a challenge, flying into wind is important but then you find the model is climbing, but reducing power lowers the speed and allows the plane to be blown backwards. In the days of single channel, rudder only models the answer to this problem was to 'S' turn the model upwind, not allowing the nose to rise and the model to climb. With the motor controlled ARTF's the turning response is not fast enough to carry out this manoeuvre.

Conclusions

We shouldn't expect too much from the low cost R/C aeroplanes. Unlike small electric cars, motorcycles and boats they have to perform in three dimensions and for the absolute beginner it is a case of being a semi-proficient pilot on the first flight, there is no question of looking at the instructions halfway through the flight. Two things will improve the chances of success enormously, to have an experienced modeller to help with the initial flying - and the ability to wait for really calm weather.

Remember that other toys will be operating on 27mHz frequencies so check that they are not on the same spot frequency as your aeroplane (if you can determine the frequency). If you want to fly more than one of the models at a time you can normally purchase them on two or three alternative frequencies, bear this in mind if you are buying them with a friend.

REVIEW - Ripmax Spitfire 600EP

The whole world of aeromodellers wants to build a Supermarine Spitfire at sometime during their hobby life, unfortunately many of the R/C model designs have either been too expensive, or were poor flyers. Small models of Spitfires, in particular were difficult to fly and prone to tip stalling - not what you want on the landing approach. Then along comes the Ripmax Spitfire, which defies convention and proceeds to perform extremely well and within the capabilities of a modeller with experience of an advanced trainer model.

Much of the success of this model can be traced to the accurate built-up structure, which results in a light and true airframe. The wing is in one piece, saving the problems of joining two panels and possibly getting them out of alignment and the fuselage has integral wing fairings (often omitted on model 'Spits') and the mount for the 600 class electric motor. A full set of control linkages, spinner, cowling, a canopy, tailsurfaces and an Instruction Manual completes the package. Covering is Oracover, a genuine heatshrink film, with the camouflage and markings printed on the surface. How the factory operatives, in China, manage to cover these semi-scale models so accurately I don't know, but Johnny Johnson's Spitfire really looks great.

Watch out for

When I did the original review of the Ripmax Spitfire I couldn't resist modifying it to IC power. There were two reasons for this departure, the main one being my love of a little noise and smell from models and the other that it would be possible to shorten the nose and make it even

more 'Spit' like. The conversion, fitting an elderly O.S. 20FS engine, was entirely successful and required a minimum of adaptation; it was almost designed for the change.

No problems were encountered in the general assembly, when cutting away the central covering on the tailplane, for gluing it the fuselage, it should not be assumed that the markings on the covering can be taken as accurately defining the centre line - measure! When fitting the elevator and rudder pushrods remember that they cross over in the fuselage and will exit on the opposite side to the servo. You must ensure that you get a sound and strong soldered joint between the pushrods and the adapters; to achieve this strip the white plastic covering away from the wire to the depth of the adapter recess, place the wire end into the adapter with the threaded end upwards. Apply heat to the adapter and solder to the open end below and you will find that, once the heat melts the solder, that it will be sucked into the orifice. This capillary action ensures that the solder is taken into the adapter, but give a good tug after the solder has set to test the strength.

Flight Qualities

Although the initial review tests were carried out with the IC version of the Spitfire I have witnessed many EP models fly and have flown some of them myself. With the powerful brushless motors and Li-po batteries there is no lack of urge with the EP Spitfire, certainly the equivalent of the IC versions; in fact, any more power and it might prove too much of a strain on the lightweight airframe.

Hand-holds are included in the underside of the wing, you only have to cut the film away, but a good hand launcher will not need them and they can be left fully covered. From the launch the Spitfire smoothed into the air and it was rapidly obvious that she was as much a thoroughbred as the full-size aircraft. All the fears of having a twitchy, barely controllable model vanished and it was immediately possible to enjoy the flying. After a few relatively gentle manoeuvres the controls were explored in a more vigorous manner, performing very 'Spit' like loops and barrel rolls. The controls are nicely harmonised, but the rudder is not over effective; stall turns are not great, you could opt to omit the rudder control, there is no undercarriage fitted so no worries about take-off swings.

Conclusions

A fine flying Spitfire at an economic price, suitable for low cost 600 motors and NiMh 9.6 volt batteries, or more exotic electric packages, or '20' to '26' size IC motor conversions. There are also due to be P-51D and a Messerschmitt Bf109 models in the same range.

Specifications

Distributor	Ripmax
Wing Span	1200mm (48ins)
Weight	1.45kg (3.2lbs)
Motor	600 series
Functions	3 to 4 channel
RRP	£69.99 (2006)

JE J
JE J

ARC Ready 2 Landplane and waterplane

Various forms of materials and construction are used for ARTF models powered by IC motors. Models from the Italian company ARC are fully moulded from a range of ABS materials. This allows them to design models with flowing curves for the injection moulded components, as exemplified in their Ready 2 fuselage, fin and rudder, whose flying surfaces are also moulded, but with a foam plastic core. Similar methods are employed on the float sets and the total investment involved in tooling costs for these injection mouldings is very considerable.

Obvious from the moment of opening the large box is the quality of the mouldings and the other accessories, which include the fuel tank, spinner, wheels, metal clevises, closed loop wire for the rudder and even a special long screwdriver for the undercarriage - and a large sheet of decals. Instructions are well illustrated, don't be fazed by the apparent complications, it all becomes obvious with the parts to hand. The float kit for the Ready 2 comes in two parts, the float set and the float fittings set; you will need both for this model, although the floats can be used on other models. Standards and qualities of the flat sets are equally good and the fittings sets are also available for the ARC Cessna 177 and DH Beaver.

Watch our for

It is important to make a decision of whether the Ready 2 is to be flown off water before you start assembly as you will need a more powerful engine with the floats fitted. A 0.40 is sufficient for the landplane, but something around a 0.46 - 50 size

engine is needed for the extra weight of the floats and the resistance of the water. Before finalising the fitting of the engine check the relative positions of the engine silencer and the front float supports, you may need to cant the engine, or use a different silencer, to miss the strut. Engineering standards are such that thin cyano can be used for joining firewalls, formers and other injection moulded items, just like a plastic kit. Where epoxy is the required adhesive make sure that you remove any surplus glue before it sets, some epoxies tend to discolour in time and look unsightly. Follow the instructions to the letter and you shouldn't have any problems with the assembly.

Flight Qualities

At a stated weight of 2800gms which equated to the review model within a few grams, the Ready 2 is somewhat heavier than many of the '40' size trainers, sufficiently so to give a little concern for the initial test flight. We need not have worried, ARC have done their homework and thanks to the efficient wing the only difference is that the flying speed is a little higher. Although the nosewheel seems a little wobbly it is perfectly strong enough, even when flying from roughish grass. The stall is totally predictable and it takes persistence to get the wing, usually the left wing to drop. Crank up the control movements and the model is quite aerobatic, a fair amount of down elevator was required for level inverted flight and she will spin, taking 1 to 2 turns to recover depending on how much you let it wind-up. Low speed handling is good, which makes the approaches for landing comfortable and the elevator authority is sufficient at the round-out for touch-down. With the floats fitted the weight had increased to over 7lbs and again we wondered whether the flying qualities would deteriorate. The optional water rudder works fine and allows accurate positioning of the model, even in moderately windy conditions. Opening up the throttle the Ready 2 tracks straight and when flying speed is reached, with the floats already up on the step, up elevator will lift her clear of the water. In very calm conditions it might be necessary to carry out some fast taxiing to cause a few ripples on the water in the area of the take-off. Once in the air the flight characteristics are not that different to the wheeled version, the entry to the spin is more pronounced and if you want a real thrill try an inverted spin - but from a safe height. Landing approaches remain steady, but the real challenge and satisfaction is getting the touchdown exactly right, without any bounce or attitude change.

Conclusions

The Ready 2 is used as the standard trainer for some of the Model Flying Schools due to its rugged qualities and interchangeable spares. For waterplane work the moulded plastic is ideal, as there is no deterioration of the materials in the water.

Specification

Distribution	Ripmax
Wing Span	62ins (1570mm)
Length	43ins (1090mm)
Weight	6lbs 4oz (2800gms)
Engine	40-53 two stroke
Radio	4 channel, four or five servos
RRP	£89.99 (2006)

Floats

Length	33-1/2ins (850mm)
RRP	Floats £42.50, Fittings Set £7.99, Water Rudder £7.99

REVIEW - Cermark Graduate

Having experienced the delights of a first solo and gone on to learn the basics of R/C flying it is time to move on to a model capable of giving a more aerobatic performance, but remaining within the abilities of the pilot. You need to explore the envelope of the model and also learn to get into - and out of - all the positions a model can achieve, only then will you be a fully qualified R/C pilot.
The low wing 'Graduate' model, now with a fully symmetrical wing aerofoil, is not only a design suitable for this second step in flying training, it is also a most attractive aeroplane and will be enjoyed just as much by the more advanced sports flyer.
As befits an ARTF the structural components are ready built and covered, with Ultracote heat shrink material and the standards of materials and workmanship are consistently high. Included in the package are the fuel tank, wheels, spinner, cowling and linkage accessories, everything you need apart from the engine, radio equipment, some fuel tubing and a little patience.

Watch out for

The instructions are abysmal, apart from one line drawing of the servo and linkage connection disposition and some poor quality linkage photographs in the correction sheet; there is no assembly illustration. I know that this kit is for intermediate level flyers, but why make it more difficult than necessary.
No measurements are given for the length of the nose wheel leg; it should be fitted so that there is a slight positive angle of attack (the wing leading edge a touch higher than the trailing edge) when the model is sitting on the ground. 'Install the fuel tank behind the firewall', states the instructions, No, the fuel tank can only be positioned as far as the intermediate former between the firewall and

the former immediately in front of the wing seating; you will need 6ins (150mm) lengths of fuel tubing to reach the carburettor, silencer pressure nipple and fill line. The engine mount is supplied as two 'T' arms, with strengthening webs, but no indication of which way up to secure the mounts. They should be fixed with the webs at the top. Holes in the firewall for the mounts are not centralised; you must make the width adjustments to allow for this.

Pre-cut holes for the nosewheel steering and engine throttle linkage tubes are not large enough. It is possible to enlarge those for the nosewheel steering, with a round file, but it is difficult to access the intermediate hole for the throttle tube, you may have to fit an alternative linkage of a smaller diameter. There is a tendency for the pushrod dowels to split when the metal rods are attached, drill carefully and bind and glue securely before fitting the heat shrink tubing.

Flight Qualities

The old adage of 'if it looks right it will fly well' certainly applies here. The Graduate will do everything an intermediate trainer should do and do it with style. Ground handling with the tricycle undercarriage and steerable nosewheel is very good; the take-off straight and the climb-out only needed a touch of down elevator to trim it out. She handles a wind well and a '40' size two-stroke glow engine gives ample power to try those aerobatic manoeuvres which couldn't be performed with a basic trainer. The stall is benign

after numerous landings, the end of the nosewheel leg should be de-burred so that it fits the hole in the steering arm. Bends have not been made in the pushrod wires, as stated, don't try to do these with pliers, use a vice to obtain a good right angle bend. The nylon keepers are a tight fit, drill the hole in the servo arm when it is out of the model and fit the keep before the arm is secured to the servo, it is a tight fit.

Flight qualities

No problems here, the Arrow, as befits its name, flew straight and true. The symmetrical wing section puts the models into the realms of a basic trainer cum intermediate trainer, it is certainly capable of performing aerobatics to a higher level than you would achieve with the average flat bottom wing model, this is certainly so if an engine at the top of the range is fitted. When the 'Arrow' is being used as an ab-initio trainer it would be sensible to have the guidance of an instructor and, if possible, a dual control system until a safe solo stage is reached. It is not a difficult model to fly, but a little faster and more powerful, a benefit for less than ideal weather conditions but like a powerful sports car, not to be treated lightly.

Conclusions

The manual covers all aspects of the preparation for assembly and flight thoroughly, although the illustrations for checking the balance are unconvincing - use a proper means of checking the balance. A Glossary of Terms is also useful, particularly for the beginner and the checking of control movements is well explained. How many instruction manuals tell you how many rubber bands to use to secure the wing, how to arrange them and how to look after them when they are removed? Very little is missing from this competent kit, flying instructions are not included, they would obviously prefer you to take the sensible and safe route of receiving help from a club, or experienced R/C flyer.

Specifications

Distributor	Helger Flight
Wing span	63in (1600mm)
Length	52.5in (1334mm)
Wing area	710sq.in (45.8sq.dm)
Weight	5.5 - 6.0lb (2.49 - 2.72kg)
Review model	6lb 5oz (2.88kg)
Engines	0.40 - 46 2-stroke, 0.56 - 0.72 4-stroke
Radio	4 channels – R, E, M, A

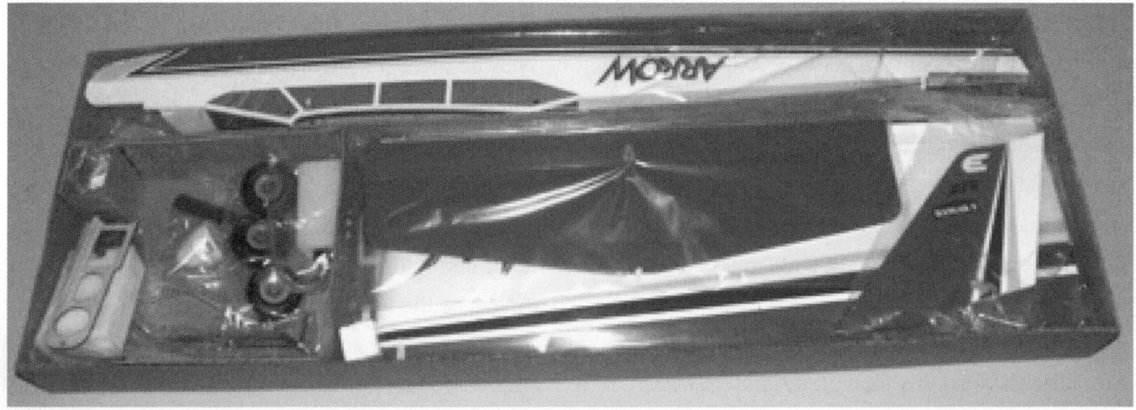

REVIEW - VMAR A-4 Skyhawk

For those of us who cannot afford, or do not wish to operate, gas turbine powered models the alternative is to fly semi-scale jets powered by IC engines. The VMAR Skyhawk is based on the American McDonnell Douglas A-4 'Bantam Bomber', it has a good layout and lends itself to having an engine at the nose, providing that sufficient weight can be concentrated at the rear to obtain the correct C of G. Two decorated versions are produced, the 'Blue Angels' example reviewed here and a less colourful, light grey, US Navy aircraft model.

Lift the lid off the highly impressive box and you are confronted with well protected and packed items, the airframe components being covered in the Vcote 2-3DS system where all the markings are printed in the heat-shrink material but, not being on the surface, it is completely fuel proof. The Skyhawk kit is very complete, with all the necessary hardware and accessories, neatly bagged and labelled, an aluminium spinner is a nice touch, as are the metal hub wheels and undercarriage legs with dummy oleos.

Watch out for

Retracts are optional and because there are many types no information is given on fitting them. Unless you fly from hard runways it would be advisable to save weight and forego the retracts and the pre-wired tip lights, which need a separate battery. The Instruction Manual is precise and illustrated with colour photos; it covers all aspects of the assembly and preparation for flight - but not in the detail you would expect for a simpler model.

Metal clevises are used on the pushrods and the gap between the arms is not sufficient for many of the servo output arms - and the supplied horns.I would prefer the simple nylon clevis at one end and 'Z' bend at the opposite end, for the aileron pushrods. As recommended, a VMAX 52 two-stroke was fitted, it is a bit of a 'shoehorn' job getting it into the nose but it does fit, although there is little room for adjusting the position and the spinner might be a little proud. Note that the

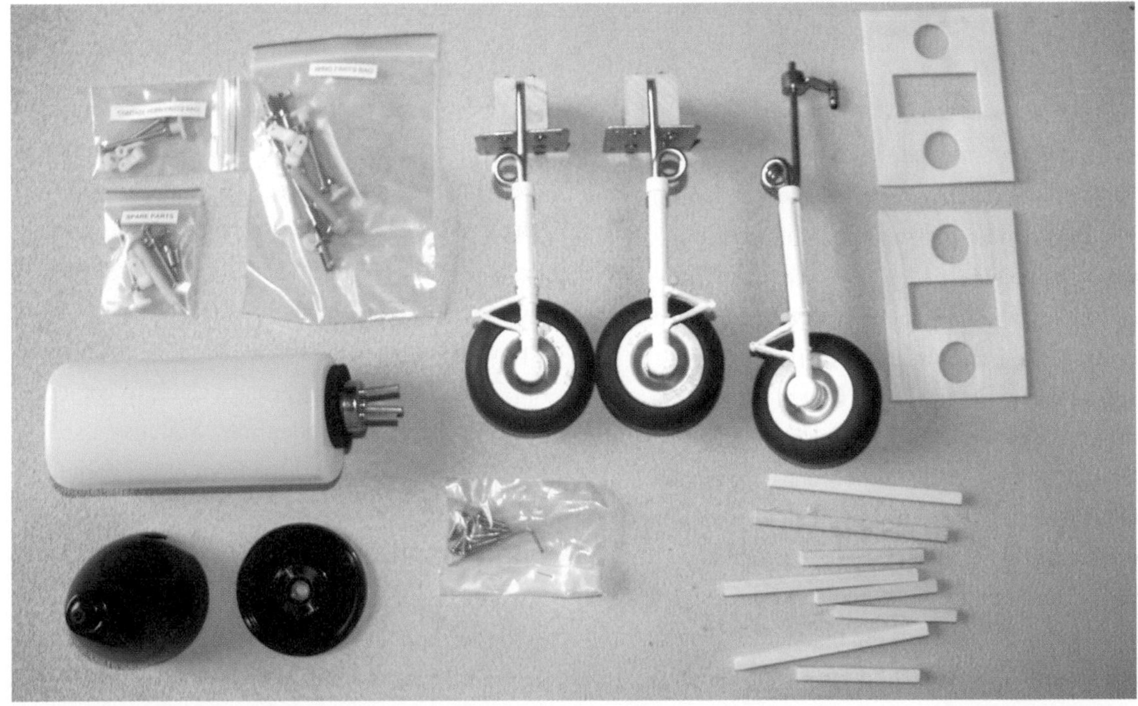

fuel tank does not locate hard up to the firewall, it stops at an intermediate former. You will need long fuel tubes to reach the engine, silencer and filler. Getting the bolts located to hold down the clamping plate (a 'part-picker' helps here) and installing the nose gear are both zero tolerance areas. It maybe necessary to trim away a little balsawood to get full movement of the steering arm; have patience, it will all work. All of the control linkages are pre-fitted and I found that the nose wheel steering rods were about an inch too short, I overcame this problem by soldering a brass connector onto the servo end and fitting a clevis. It was also a tight fit at the opposite end of the fuselage and the bends on the elevator linkage rods were insufficient to align it to the servo output. Increasing the bend angles resulted in the overall lengths being effectively reduced and longer nylon clevises had to be fitted to reach the elevator horns. To keep weighty items at the rear the battery (a flat pack 600mAh battery with AA type cells) is wedged next to the rudder extension rod. Trim the balsa longerons a shade to get it in and fit it before the rudder horn. You may also have to shave a little off the front of the horn for the screw to reach the rod.

Flight qualities

It would be nice to report that the Skyhawk took to the air without any corrections needed - at least the balance point was on the button - but life isn't

always like that, even for a reviewer. The VMAX 52 was given a run to get it bedded down and putting out full power. We were flying from our sports field flying site, in autumn and the grass wasn't all that short, but taxi trials suggested that there was sufficient urge to reach flying speed so the Skyhawk was taxied back and re-fuelled. On the take-off run, into wind, the model didn't show any inclination to lift-off and as she was making rapidly towards an earth bank I throttled back; at that point the A-4 decided to get airborne and there we were, at low speed, heading for the bank. The encouraging thing was that it didn't stall but wallowed, nose up, into the bank, knocking back the nose wheel. After repairs the Skyhawk was taken out for another attempt, this time with more elevator movement, but again it showed a disinclination to rotate and lift-off until I eventually throttled back because she was getting quite distant. This time, when it lifted, I decided to pile on the power and try to stay in the air, resulting in a rapid flick-roll into the ground and substantial damage to the fuselage.

The following day, by sheer coincidence, I heard from another modeller reviewing the same kit model that he had similar difficulties in taking off from grass - and had aborted over a dozen attempts. Frustrated, he took the model to RAF Valley, where there are acres of hard runways and was successful in getting the model airborne and flying the Skyhawk in a jet-like fashion. He claims that it was a very pleasant model to fly and that the approaches and landings were particularly rewarding.

Conclusions

Why didn't it take-off? Checking the balance point after the attempts I found that the main wheels were three inches behind the recommended location and at this distance, plus the effective downwards moment from the engine and the drag on the wheels from the grass all conspired to prevent lift-off. I would suggest, as a partial remedy, bending the main undercarriage legs forward this will reduce the distance from the wheels to the balance point and allow an easier rotation, also the main undercarriage legs will be effectively shorter giving the model a greater angle of attack. Ideally, though, operate from hard runways and allow the Skyhawk to fly itself off the ground.

Specifications

Wing span	43ins (1100mm)
Wing area	590sq.ins (38sq.dm)
Length	53ins (1350mm)
Weight	6.4 to 7.05lbs (2.9 to 3.3kg)
Engine	0.46 to 0.52cu.ins two-stroke only
Radio	4 - 6 channels (5 to 7 servos)
RRP	£149.95

REVIEW - Multiplex Easy Star

Two hours from opening the box to flying the model claims the box art of the Easy Star and it is not far wrong, although you may wish to spend a little more time on thoroughly reading the instructions and applying the decals. With a pusher-mounted motor and propeller the fully moulded model is a practical layout. The radio equipment is fully installed and the transmitter (35MHz) and charger (12 volt) supplied. Note that the moulded foam parts are from Elapor and not Styrofoam and that cyano adhesive is appropriate in this instance. The three channel Hitec Ranger 3 transmitter can be powered by eight AA dry cells or rechargeable batteries, a charging socket is provided. Two single axis sticks, with trims, are augmented by a top mounted throttle lever, two Adjustable Travel Volumes (ATV) are included, together with servo reversing and mixing facilities, the latter is not required for the Easy Star. A narrow band four channel receiver is fitted onboard the model together with a Multicont X-08 speed controller.

Watch out for

Although quite comprehensive, the instructions make no mention of fitting the wings to the fuselage. Check the fit of the carbon fibre tube spar into the moulded wings first, insert one wing panel into the fuselage, followed by the opposite panel and the spar; ensure that the panels are fully pushed home. Because the fit is very tight and you may want to remove the wings for transportation, do not glue the wings to the fuselage.

The ends of the pianowire pushrods should be

straight. Undo the grub screws in the horn connectors before fitting the tail surfaces and ensure that the elevator pushrod is positioned above the tailplane when it is fitted. Check the direction of the servos; it is quite likely they will be moving in the wrong direction, Figures A to F mentioned in the instructions are not shown; you will find similar information in this book dealing with basic aerodynamics. Because of upgrading of the kit the 12 volt peak charger was a new type. No problem, just read the new instructions included with the charger.

Decal application can be tricky due to the concave surface of the outer wings, use the soapy water method advocated in this book, but remember to press them down again after a day or two. When fitting the canopy hatch simply press it down into position, don't squeeze the sides of the canopy when doing this or the catches will not engage properly.

Whether you solder on gold plated connectors for the battery/speed controller link will depend on whether you have other electric models sharing batteries and receivers, they are recommended. No separate on/off switch is fitted. Ready to go? One final top-up charge and off to the flying field.

Flight qualities

The Easy Star looks like a practical, no nonsense trainer style model and so it proved to be. From the moment of launch - no undercarriage with this bird - it was steady and predictable in flight. No ailerons either, but turns did not result in a major wing drop, or nose down plummet, it was very regulated and controllable. Loops are possible,

but the Easy Star is not intended to be an agile circus performer, it is there to teach you, as safely as possible, the rudiments of R/C flying and this it will do if you give it half a chance. Don't expect long flight times, it is operating at high throttle settings for most of the time and don't expect a fantastic glide; get organised for your landing approach in good time.

Conclusions

Easy Star has a proven track record and is now available in the RR (Ready for Radio) form. The Hitec receiver and transmitter and the Multiplex Tiny-S servos, the Multicont X-08 speed controller are all pre-fitted, but can be used for other models. I had some reserves about the crash resistance of the foam construction but I need not have worried, it has proven to be very resilient. Recommended as an introductory level model with a good pedigree.

Specification

Distribution	Contact Gordon Upton on 0792 1166645
Wing span	1370mm
Overall length	917mm
Fuselage length	870mm
All-up weight	400 motor/6 x AA cells approx. 680g
Wing area	approx. 24 dm.sq
Wing loading	approx. 28g/dm.sq
R/C functions	Rudder, elevator and motor

Don't be put off by the name if you are a beginner, the Aerobird is, at 54ins wing span, larger than many of the pod and boom type models and, in the sports mode with reduced control surface movements, makes a very good trainer. This is a full package system where you get the completed airframe, consisting of an injection moulded 'hard' plastic fuselage, one piece rigid foam wings with carbon fibre reinforcement to the centre, foam tail surfaces, radio equipment ready installed, 35MHz three channel transmitter (not 27MHz as indicated on the box) charging equipment and rubber bands. This package is supported with a DVD giving assembly and flying advice plus a separate written and illustrated instruction manual. The comprehensive contents allow the model to be assembled in minutes rather than hours and should be within the capabilities of the tyro modeller. Presumably the airborne radio system consists of receiver, ESC (Electric Speed Controller) and two servos, it is encased in the fuselage and is not generally accessible. The battery is removed from the front hatch for charging.

Watch out for

To test the ease of preparation for flight and the completeness of the kit the Extreme was taken on a caravan holiday, albeit one for model aeroplane enthusiasts. This was achieved, even though the DVD couldn't be played. For the absolute beginner the line drawings are on the small side and could be more detailed, more emphasis could be places on the need to charge the airborne battery first, indeed, the battery should be cycled, by running the motor until the battery is exhausted, two or three times before attempting to fly the model. The motor and batteries will then reach maximum efficiency.

There is no illustration of the top plastic tail mounting or reference to the double sided adhesive tape, although these become obvious when fixing the tailplane. The control movements are well illustrated.

Flying instructions are ambiguous, they advise

you to obtain experienced assistance if you are a beginner, but then explain how to attempt to fly on your own. The flying site diagram doesn't show the wind direction and the launching diagrams appear to show the model being launched in a banked attitude. No balance point is indicated although it is unlikely to vary from model to model.

Flight qualities

With the Aerobird fully charged, from the cigar lighter adapter in the car, or a separate 12 volt battery, carry out a final check on the controls and range. The throttle arming system, whereby you must first set low throttle before the motor will respond, is a good safety feature, the slide control on the transmitter comes easily to hand. The multi-control modes on the transmitter give you the options of more gentle flying and larger control movements for aerobatics. In the sports mode only a single elevon moves at one time and in the turn a touch of up elevator is automatically programmed, saving the trainee from having to carry out this necessary function. For the experienced pilot this up elevator effect, during turns, can be off-putting, but the experienced pilot will almost certainly be operating in the Extreme transmitter setting where this coupling no longer occurs.

Power on the standard, supplied battery is more than adequate for a take-off from short grass, or from a hand launch, which is easily accomplished. A good climb rate allows height to be fairly rapidly reached and it is then possible to switch the motor off, or reduce power and search for thermals. The control response, in sports mode is good both under power and on the efficient glide, it does require a touch of up elevator to round-out for the landing. Being finished in bright yellow, the Aerobird is easy to see and by using motor control diligently, you can expect flights exceeding ten minutes.

Flick over the switch on top of the transmitter to the Xtreme setting (it can be done during the flight) and you have a different animal, it is easy

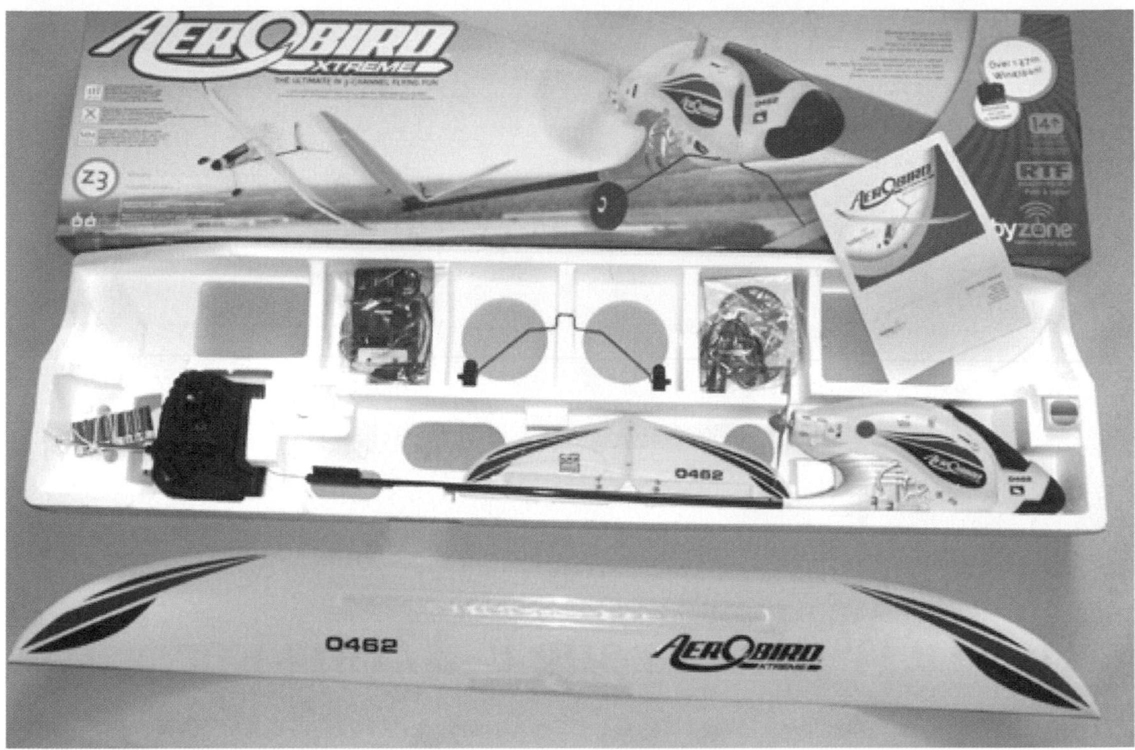

to over control the model and this will result in some Dutch rolling. Positive and measured transmitter inputs are required to track accurately through a loop and you have to be prepared to keep the nose up at the end of a roll, but it is good fun and challenging. An optional more powerful battery is available.

Conclusions

A genuine model for all seasons, the Aerobird Extreme is placid in its Sports trainer guise, but offers more experienced flyers a challenge, with the additional optional Sonic module which allows you to have combat with any other similarly equipped model (See Parkzone F-27 Stryker review).

Ignore the description of aerobatics in the manual, the 'Tailslick' is a hammer-head stall and the 'Chandelle' a stall turn, and beware of the 'Javelin' launch recommended, the Aerobird only needs a firm push. If you find that the wing is tending to move on its mounting, apply a couple of strips of wing seating tape on the top of the fuselage for a cure.

Specification

Distribution	Helger Flight Division
Wing span	54.5in (1384mm)
Wing area	304sq.in
Weight	2lbs 9oz (1162gm)
Motor (supplied)	540 can direct drive
Battery	6 x 1700mAh Nicad
RRP	£129.99 (2006)

REVIEW - Parkzone F-27 Stryker

Undoubtedly the modern lines of the F-27 Stryker will appeal to younger modellers - and not a few of the older generations too! It is by no means a difficult model to fly but it isn't a true beginners design either. In the Instruction Manual the manufacturers advise 'If you have not successfully flown one of the Hobbyzone 1 or 2 aircraft, or any other radio control aircraft, we strongly recommend that you seek the help of an experienced radio control pilot during your beginning flights'. Words of wisdom indeed. The Stryker is a smooth flyer but a little faster than the average trainer and orientation can be a problem with any flying wing model in the early piloting stages.

ARTF, in the case of the Stryker, means that all of the radio gear and linkages are installed, the transmitter is supplied, just fit eight AA batteries (supplied) and you will not need to make any more purchases before going to fly.

Watch out for

As the limits of assembly are the fitting of the nose and fins there is little to report on this area. My own preference would be to remove the double sided adhesive foam tape pieces which hold the nose in position and permanently glue (white PVA adhesive) the nose to the fuselage. The only reason for retaining the foam fixing that I can see is so that the nose, and fins, can be removed for transporting the model in its original box/carrying case.

Flying characteristics

Supplied with an 8.4 volt 900mAh NiMh battery, there is sufficient thrust for some spirited flying and power enough to get you used to the flying of the Stryker. The transmitter has a dual rate switch and it is advisable to start at the low rate for initial, smooth flying and then switch over to the higher rate for aerobatics. An optional 9.6 volt

battery pack can be purchased and if you don't want to wait for the 40 minutes needed to recharge the standard battery this would be a sensible acquisition. With no undercarriage fitted a hand launch is obligatory. It is not difficult but requires a firm, level push and the pilot should be ready with a touch of up elevator to prevent the model from sinking-out after the launch. A useful handgrip is moulded on the underside of the fuselage.

Conclusions

Would-be jet jockeys unable to afford a true jet, gas turbine powered R/C model should find solace in the Parkzone Stryker, it may have an electric motor and propeller mounted over the rear fuselage, but it really looks the part. If you haven't tried elevons (combines elevator and aileron) the diagrams in the manual will be useful and also heed the advice on flying - or not flying -

in strong winds. Also, you should fly the model like the real thing, don't try to emulate the shock flyers, this is not for sharp changes of direction, the drag will slow it down too much. If you want to increase the fun potential go for the 'X-Port' feature with the Sonic Combat Module allowing you to have 'Dog fights' with other SCM equipped models; when you get a 'hit' the other model emits a high pitched sound and the motor is cut for ten seconds, allowing them to land or prepare for a counter attack. When the firing button, positioned on top of the transmitter, is depressed it also emits a high pitched sound. It puts a new meaning on the term 'friendly fire'.

Specification

Distributed in the UK by Helger Distribution

Wing span	37ins (950mm)
Length	27ins (700mm)
Weight	21oz (580g)
Motor	480 Power direct drive
FM Radio	3 proportional channels
Battery	8.4v 900mAh Ni-MH
Charger	DC peak detect
Wing	Durable EPP foam
RRP	£139.99

REVIEW - Thunder Tiger, Tiger Trainer 40

Thunder Tiger were among the first companies to produce good quality, reasonably priced, comprehensively kitted ARTF trainers and the classic Tiger Trainer 40 results from a line of designs starting with the Skylark 40. Advances and improvements in manufacturing techniques have brought about a number of changes over the years, but the basic design parameters have remained the same. The aim has always been to produce a model that 'features state-of-the-art engineering that provides quick and easy assembly of a strong, yet lightweight aeroplane that will provide you with an enjoyable and educational experience.'

Kit contents are commendably complete for this 40 to 46 powered basic trainer, construction is primarily from balsawood and plywood. The airframe is film covered but the fuselage top decking and the wing and tailsurface tips have moulded plastic finishes, the engine cowling is a two piece injection moulding. A 28 page Instruction Manual is equally comprehensive, it takes you, stage by stage, through all the areas of assembly, installations and preparation for flight; it really does take you by the hand and spell out, in words of one syllable, to the stage of being ready for flight. All the kit parts are fully identified in the manual, making it easy to check whether anything is missing - there wasn't.

Watch out for

One penalty of constantly updating the manufacturing and design of a model is that the Instruction Manual does not always keep pace with the alterations and this has been the case with the Tiger Trainer. Such items as the servo tray being pre-fitted and not supplied separately,

as shown in the manual, is of no particular consequence, but when the engine mount is of entirely different form the manual should reflect this change. It is now a three part item and no indication is given, pictorially or in words, how it is to be fitted. Oddly, the new engine mount set is correctly illustrated in the parts sketches. When fitting the mount remember that the strengthening webs go at the top of the mount. The nose gear steering arm linkage does not go under the fuselage, as shown in the manual, it is routed within the cowling. An extra collet (collar) is needed to restrain the nosewheel leg and the coil spring must be low enough to clear the skirt on the cowling, or the skirt cut away. A small amount (3/8in, 10mm) must also be cut from the rear top opening on the cowling to clear the engine cylinder and the cowling must be fitted before the engine is screwed to the bearers, the cowling will not fit over the engine if that is fitted first. Test fit the engine and ensure you have a dimension of 4-1/4ins (107mm) from the firewall to the front of the prop-driver. Although the same fuel tank is shown in the parts list and in the photographs it will not fit in the spaces cut into the front fuselage formers. If you cut away the formers sides it will affect the holes for the linkage tubes, it is simpler to fit an alternative fuel tank. The only problem encountered in the radio and linkage installations was the pushrod connectors. The unthreaded part of the spigot was not long enough to clear the servo output arm and the nut tightened onto the arm, preventing the connector from turning, and the metal clevises specified where actually nylon types. Pushrods were already made-up.

Before you finalise the battery location check the

balance point, I found that it was correct with the battery under the servos and the receiver immediately in front of them.

Flight qualities

Tiger Trainers have been used by professional flying schools, a tribute to both the flying qualities and the robust standards of the model. The flat bottom wing section does not seem to inhibit its good flying abilities in windier conditions and the tendency to 'balloon' i.e. for the nose to come up, after a diving turn is little greater than a trainer with a symmetrical wing section. The fact that it is a high lift section means that it can be slowed up more without stalling. Tricycle undercarriages certainly make for easier tracking on take-off and the steerable nosewheel works well, even on grass. In addition to teaching you the basics of flying, the Tiger Trainer 40 is quite capable of putting you through the basic aerobatic schedule, it is both forgiving and manoeuvrable. Number 64 rubber bands are specified for holding the wing in position, 7ins (180mm) bands seem about right, too, if you are using thick white types four bands should suffice - plus one for the wife and one for the kids!

Conclusions

Experienced modellers will have no problems in assembling the 'Tiger Trainer 40', but this is intended as a basic trainer and the omissions in the otherwise excellent Instruction Manual could be worrisome to a first time builder of an ARTF kit. It is not easy to get practical help and assistance if you live in remote areas. If you are unsure of any areas of assembly ask for advice from the retailer - another good reason for purchasing kits from bona fide model shops. Once assembled you have a good standard trainer and the Thunder Tiger 42GP engine will give ample power for that

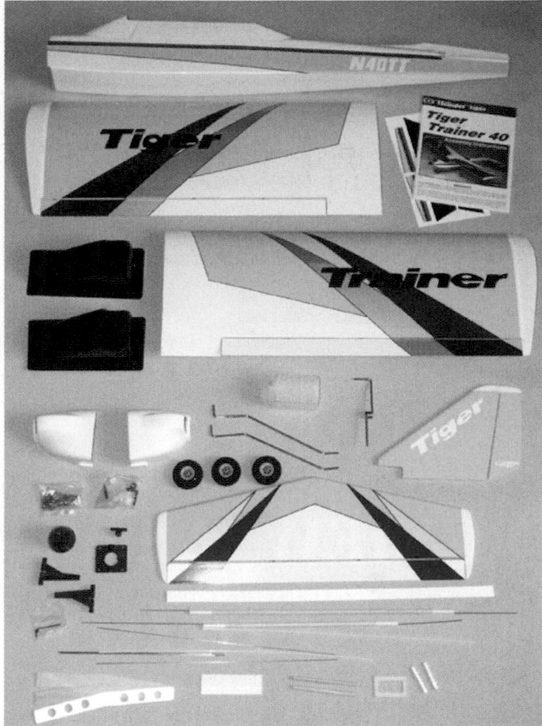

purpose, if you want a more sporty model, the PRO46 will give that extra urge. The 40 size trainer is large enough to see easily and to have authority in the air, but there is a larger, 60 version (1850mm wing span) if you prefer big models.
It is good to know that some models improve with age and the gradual improvements with the TT 40 model, plus the advantages of computer radios such as the Hitec Optic 6, makes this classic design better than ever.

Specification

Distributor	Messrs Amerang
Wing span	1549mm
Length	1295mm
IC Engine	0.40 to 0.46
Radio	4 channels 4 servos
RRP	£69.99 (2006)

REVIEW - Multiplex Twin Star II

The original Twin Star must be one of the most successful ARTF electric models ever manufactured, certainly the most successful twin motor model, they have been produced in their tens of thousands. I have seen them raced, flown in combat, slope soared, aerobatted, carrying cameras, touch and go on land (wet grass) and even on water and on one occasion a dowel was strapped to the top wing and doughnuts were transported from a cliff to the beach below! Mostly, though, it was used as an excellent sports model, capable of giving great satisfaction and pleasure to its owner. Multiplex have now brought out a Mark 2 version of this popular design, incorporating improvements in assembly methods and structural integrity.

First impressions on picking up the well illustrated box was to doubt that the supposed contents, including the airframe, motors, linkages and accessories, could really be all there, the box seemed too light. A clever twist to the design of the box is to have the accessories, separately boxed, secured in a cutout in one corner, I'll swear that the box manufacturers have degrees in Origami. Yes, everything is there and for you to make absolutely certain that this is so the Instruction Manual has numbered line drawings and lists relating to the parts to ensure that every part can easily be identified. In fact the Manual is an example of how instructions should be written (in five languages) and illustrated; yes, some of the writings are the same as those used in other Multiplex productions but, why not, the differences are fully and clearly described.

For those of you unaware of the methods used in the Multiplex models such as the Easy Star, Magister and Twin Star 2, the airframes are manufactured from moulded foam components, not the more usual Styrofoam but a material called Elapor, it may look the same as Styrofoam, but it isn't. For starters you use standard cyano for gluing the parts together and it is also tough. How do I know? I had the misfortune of having a faulty aileron servo extension lead result in the Magister model I was flying do a violent wingover into the ground; it survived with remarkably little damage. Hard points, for wing

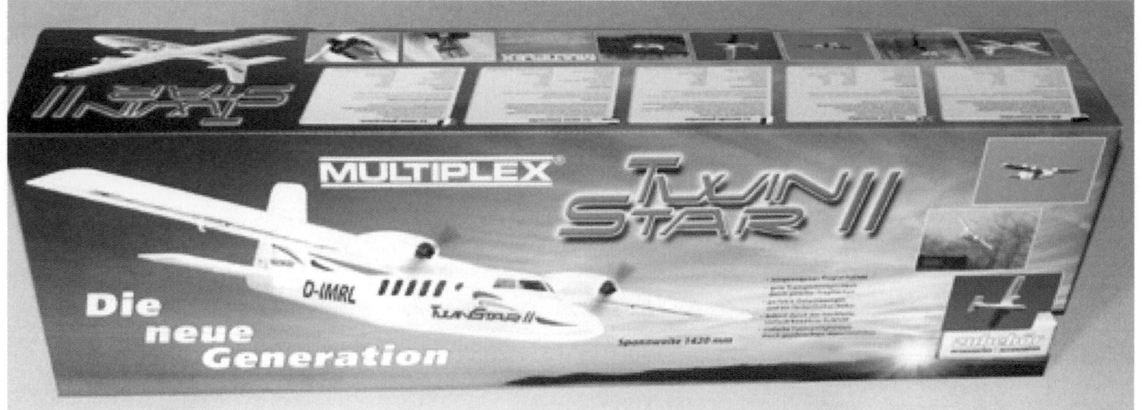

fixings, are formed with injection moulded plastic parts which are glued to the structures. Cyano adhesive, the scourge of Styrofoam is the correct glue to use on Elapor, the general technique being to spray the activator onto only one surface and the cyano onto the other mating part, you then bring the two components rapidly together. Hot-melt glue can be used for fixing servos, or epoxy and the radio parts, including the battery are held in position with Velcro style hook and loop tapes. Permax 400 motors are included, together with the mounts, propellers and power leads; also included is a neat connector board which can be used as a terminal for the motor power leads and aileron servo connections for easy assembly at the flying field. All of the control horns and control linkages are supplied and the package is completed with a colourful decal set. You will have to provide the adhesives, receiver, four mini servos, 300mm extension leads, a 32.35amp speed controller and a 7 or 8 cell 2/300mAh NiMH battery.

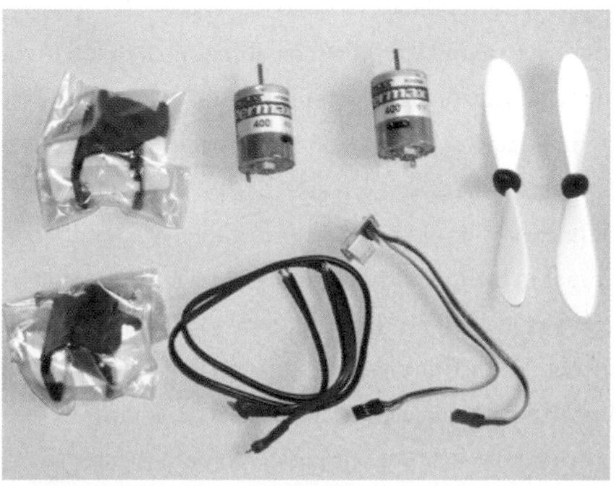

Watch out for

Fits of moulded components are precise and with the adhesives being mostly of the instant variety there is no waiting about for the glue to dry. One area where the instant glue can be a problem is with the fitting of the fin and rudder, if you apply the cyano to all of the surfaces and activator to the mating surfaces you may find that the adhesive 'grabs' before the fin can be pushed fully home, a slower drying adhesive is recommended for this operation. All moulded foam components have small dimple marks on the surface, these can be left in the condition they are when released from the mould, or they can be smoothed down with fine, but sharp abrasive paper, it will help to keep the decals flat when they are applied. Follow the instructions precisely and you shouldn't come across any major problems, I did find that the quoted length of the rudder linkage inner tube was a tad too long, reduce it from 705mm to 700mm. Naturally, the Twin Star 2 is designed with Multiplex radio in mind, but any of the standard outfits can be used, the servos have to be mini sized, those for the rudder and elevator should not be more than 15mm wide or it will be impossible to fit the battery. Because I was moving radio equipment from one model to another,

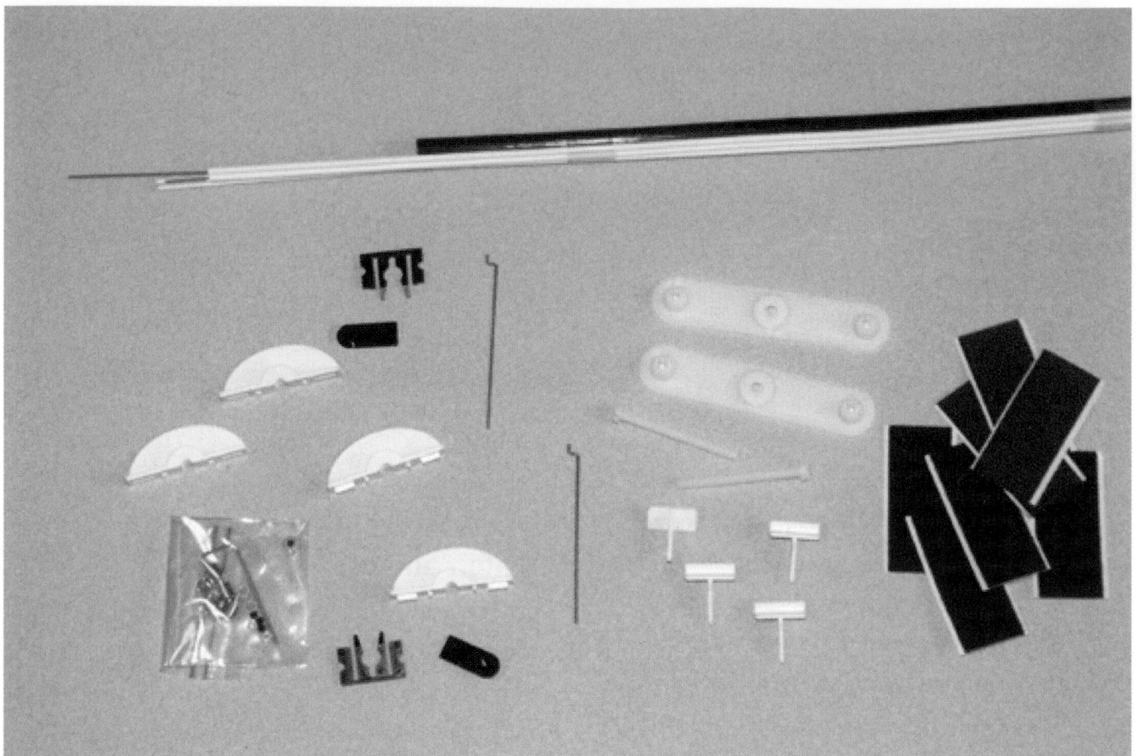

for review purposes, I fixed the servos in position with double-sided adhesive tape, but epoxy, or hot-melt glue would give a more permanent adhesion. Pre-formed aileron pushrods are only just long enough to reach the horn connector, so slope the output arms slightly towards the ailerons to keep the distance acceptable, remember that the servo output arm screw must be fixed before the servo is glued in position. An extension is required for the aileron servo leads and if a standard plug and socket extension lead is used you will have to cut away a fair amount of the internal foam channel to allow for the bulk of the plug and socket. A neater solution is to release the connectors on the servo plug, discard the plug casing and solder to the connectors a servo/battery lead of a suitable length, remember to slip on lengths of heat-shrink tube for protection of the joint. When gluing the motor and servo leads into the wing trough note that the leads should be positioned with the wires vertically stacked and not laid horizontally, this will allow the spar covers to fit without any further trimming. Before gluing the covers permanently in position do check that the motors are running in the correct directions, fit the propellers to check the draught and that the aileron servos are working correctly.

When cutting away the surplus foam around the engine nacelles cut as close to the nacelle as possible to avoid the little tabs of foam being left and which are difficult to remove - use 240 grade sanding paper, as for the other foam surfaces. The large decal sheet is rolled and to get it flat again tape, in three or four places, the edge of the sheet and wrap it in the reverse direction around a cardboard tube and leave it for 30 minutes or so, it should then lay flat. Battery leads terminate with three pin plugs, they can be connected to the connector board in any order, no instructions are given with regard to gluing the board in position and because the plugs are a very tight fit it is preferable to leave the board loose.

To obtain the required balance point an eight cell 2000 or 3000mAh battery must be positioned rearwards under the wing, with the connectors to the speed controller to the front. Even with the battery pushed hard back the balance point is marginally forward, mark the location for any other sized batteries e.g. seven celled or LiPos.

Flight qualities

Many compliments have been made of the flying qualities of the Twin Star and these qualities follow through to the Mark 2 version. In its standard form, with a 2000 or 3000mAh battery pack and seven or eight cells the performance is more than respectable and will satisfy most modellers, in particular those experiencing electric flight, or R/C flying in general, for the first time. There is sufficient urge to get the Twin Star safely to height from the hand launch (remember, no undercarriage) and the model is sufficiently forgiving to allow it to be thrown around without the worry of it doing anything untoward, the stall is benign. Mild aerobatics come within its repertoire and are satisfying, ensure that the battery is well secured with the Velcro style tape. She is no slouch and can be flown in windier conditions but for most enjoyment and precision low level flying a calm day will give the utmost satisfaction. Power-off gliding is acceptable, but don't get caught out low down and far out through exceeding a safe flying time, the temptation to continue flying is considerable.

Conclusions

An updated version of a very popular electric twin retaining the excellent values of the original and including improvements on the assembly and structural strength. The wings can be retained as separate panels, I preferred to join them for convenience, it is a little 'fiddly' plugging in the motor and aileron servo leads. You will notice from the control surface travels that aileron differential movement is specified, the easiest way to obtain this is by having the aileron servos plugged into independent outputs on the receiver, but you will need a six channel receiver and a computerised transmitter for this purpose. If you only have a four channel system you can overcome this problem by going back to basic geometry and installing the servo output so that the take off for the pushrod is offset towards the front of the wing, this will give more up aileron than down. To achieve this you will have to make longer pianowire pushrods, alternatively you can use the standard 'Y' lead connector, set the ailerons up by about 3/32in and work harder at co-ordinating the turns with aileron and rudder.

Perhaps you will be tempted to increase the performance of the Twin Star 2 by using three cell (11.1 volt) Li-Po batteries. The supplied 6 volt 400 canned motors are not really rated for this and unless you limit the power cautiously you could burn out the motors; a better alternative would be to fit brushless motors of similar size and mountings. Judging by the excellent performance with the standard motors and an eight cell 2000 or 3000mAh battery pack, I doubt whether many Twin Star 2 owners will bother to change the status quo.

Specifications

Distributor UK	Gordon Upton 0792 1166645
Wing span	1420mm (56ins)
Length	1085mm (43ins)
Wing area	43dm.sq. (4.7sq.ft)
Weight	1500gms (53oz)
Wing loading	35g/dm.sq. (11.5oz/sq.ft)
Radio	4 - 6 channel, 5 mini servos
RRP	£69.95

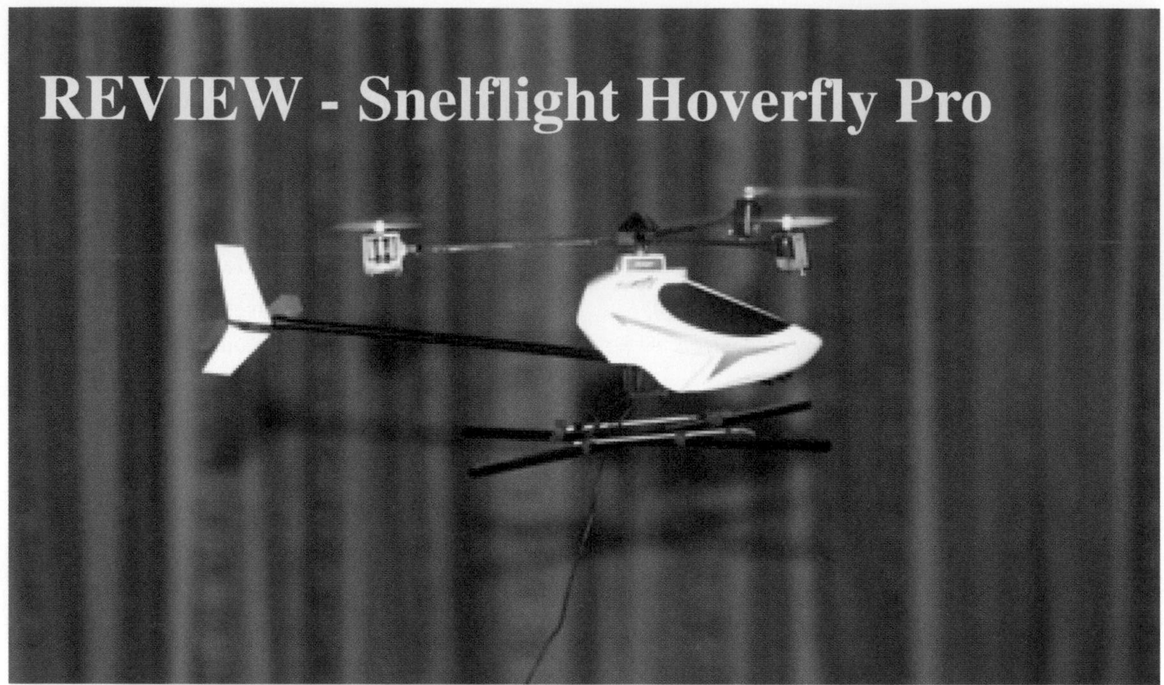

Can you really get any idea of flying a 'real' helicopter by experimenting with a small indoor model, powered from the mains via an umbilical cord and costing less than £50.00? The answer is 'Yes' and the Snelflight Hoverfly is capable of reproducing the control reactions of a normal, free flying helicopter with cyclic control. For this cost you must supply your own transmitter, all the popular makes are compatible with the Hoverfly Pro, but comes complete with a small, lightweight helicopter, mains lead, Electrocyclic Control Processor, transmitter signal lead, decals, spares and a comprehensive instruction manual, part of which is quoted in the introduction to helicopter flying.

By employing lightweight components and an extremely slow rotor speed the Hoverfly is comparatively safe and suitable for indoor operation. Using small rotor-tip propellers, driven by separate motors, to generate lift, the main rotor turns only for the sake of stability. Propeller speeds respond rapidly to changes of control i.e. electrical supply and allows cyclic control during each revolution of the main rotor without needing any mechanical input; thus the swash plate and servos are eliminated. With the majority of the aircraft's mass contained in the motor at the rotor tips stability, even at low rotor speeds, mimics those of larger helicopter, while making it safe to fly indoors. The tail rotor is fixed pitch and used only for yaw control, a simple arrangement made possible because of the lack of torque reaction from the tip mounted propellers.

Watch out for

Do take the trouble of reading the extremely well written, thorough and comprehensive Instruction and Maintenance Manual, this is of particular importance if you are a newcomer to helicopter flying. Although it is possible to purchase the Hoverfly with the addition of the Lightning 4 transmitter, many would-be helicopter flyers will probably prefer to use their own transmitters so that they become familiar with the control when they move on to 'unfettered' R/C helicopters. Full instructions are given for positioning the links in the ECP and servo switches for the various makes and types of transmitters follow these precisely and you shouldn't have any problems.

Assembly of the Hoverfly is little more than fitting the training undercarriage and applying the decals. Plug in the connections from the aircraft to the ECP, to the transmitter and to the mains supply and you are ready to go.

Flight qualities

Intended primarily for beginners to helicopter flying the Hoverfly instructions for carrying out your first flight, or attempting to do so, are very thorough; it is vital to read the section on 'Your First Flight' from beginning to end before attempting to fly. For more experienced helicopter pilots it is still necessary to understand the different technique required for take-off procedures. As a novice to helicopter flying you will have no idea of how the Hoverfly compares, in control and flight, with fully equipped electric and IC powered models, for this purpose we put it in the hands of more experienced pilots. The general consensus was that it performed in a manner very similar to the 'real' helicopter models and that the control functions were faithfully followed. There is no pretence that learning to fly a conventional helicopter is easy, in comparison with the twin rotor helicopters for instance, and you are likely to crash the Hoverfly while learning. Fortunately the Hoverfly is fairly rugged and the cost of any replacement parts is low. Because of its small size it is not stable when being held on, or just above floor level and it is recommended that you move away from ground turbulence effects, to a height of at least 12ins, as soon as possible.

Conclusions

Conventional helicopter flying is never going to be easy and any help you can get in achieving safe controlled flight is worthwhile. The Snelflight Hoverfly allows you to practice the normal control of a helicopter, indoors and at a very modest cost; the fact that you are flying it in three dimensions, albeit with an umbilical cord, makes it a more versatile aid than a PC simulator. In common with learning to fly other forms of radio controlled model aircraft it will help if you have an experienced pilot to assist you, if only to ensure that the model is well trimmed.

Specifications

Manufacturer Snelflight Ltd
Churchill House, 57 Jubilee Road,
Waterlooville, Hants. PO7 7RF
Tel. 02392 258 999

Rotor diameter	284mm
Weight	68g
Power	Mains AC reduced to 34v
Radio	4 function PPM
Tip prop speed at hover	22K rpm
Price	£44.95 (2006)

REVIEW - E-Flite Tensor 4D

3D is a very popular form of R/C flying, but 4D? Strictly speaking the Tensor doesn't have a fourth dimension, even if there is one, but with a configuration that incorporates vast amounts of side area, it is purported to fly as well in knife edge as it does upright or inverted. This 'shock' flyer comes in a genuine flat pack kit, with high quality pre-printed Depron airframe components plus carbon fibre bracing rods, undercarriage, wheels and appropriately small moulded fittings. Only the adhesives, motor and electronics are not supplied. The instruction manual is very thorough and understandable, giving step-by-step instructions in words and pictures.

It would be pushing the bounds of belief to call the Tensor an attractive model. It does have a certain functionality, no doubt resulting from its aerodynamicist designer, George Hicks, aims of achieving maximum yaw authority and knife edge flight; the wing side force generators are very prominent.

Control surfaces are ready hinged, with clear adhesive tape and most of the laminating and fixing of doublers is already done. What is left is to slot the components together, glue them and add the carbon rod bracing. This is not a difficult undertaking but does require care and patience to ensure that everything is correctly aligned. 'Foam friendly' cyano adhesive is recommended for almost all of the construction, some of these glues take a long time to set when used for Depron to Depron joints, but not all of the 'kickers' (accelerators) are suitable with the paint finishes on the model; experiment first.

By reading the Assembly Manual thoroughly before commencing construction you can determine the location of the three micro servos, it will be easier to cut the openings in the Depron

sheet for them before assembly starts. From there on follow the 40 pages of instructions religiously, although you many want to omit the wheel spats if you fly from grass and you may wish to fit the Li-Po battery under the horizontal fuselage rather than on top. Bear in mind the location of the speed controller and receiver, also the routing of the leads from the motor.

Watch out for

The horizontal fuselage supports (doublers) are taped in position with double-sided thin adhesive tape. There is only need to remove one of them to fit the horizontal fuselage to the vertical piece and this should be done with great care to avoid damage, use a very sharp, long bladed knife slid between the foam sections. An outrunner motor is recommended for the Tensor, but the method of fixing to the plywood former will vary, where the former has to be glued to the front of the fuselage, with the motor behind it, the fixing should be reinforced and epoxy used in place of cyano. Ensure that the rotating case of the motor is clear of the fuselage. Micro servos have short plug leads, arrange the receiver location and select servos so that you do not need to use servo extension leads. Assembly is not difficult but does need patience and care, particularly if the adhesive is slow drying. Before the carbon fibre rod bracing is fitted the airframe is quite 'floppy' and must be handled gently, but firmly. When the assembly is completed check all the joints and reinforce with additional glue fillets.

Flight Qualities

The designer includes some very specific instructions regarding the setting up and flying of the Tensor. To get the best out of the model you certainly need a transmitter with rates and exponential functions. When fitting the ESC it is possible to connect the plugs so that the motor direction is reversed, this can lead to the model being pushed backwards so when testing restrain it in both directions. Setting-up and flying details

are very thorough and also advise would-be 3D flyers to practise hard on the simulator.

Not being an experienced 'shockie' flyer I was quite prepared to hand over the test flying to a club mate and arranged to meet him a the clubhouse to sort out frequencies for his transmitter (he flies Mode 2 and I fly Mode 1). What I wasn't prepared for was for him to opt to test fly the Tensor 4D in the adjacent room - smaller than your average village hall. That he did, successfully, albeit only in a prop-hanging style, says volumes for the flight qualities of the model and for the high standard of Lee's piloting skills. The second outing was in a larger sports hall and this gave an opportunity to test the more conventional, but extreme flight characteristics of the 'shockie'. Aerobatic manoeuvrability is immediately obvious, with the side force generators doing their job and making knife edge flight a lot easier, but requiring greater inputs of rudder for tight turns. To get the most out of the Tensor indoors you really do need to maximum control surface deflections stated in the manual and you will only get these by shortening the control horns, as per the instructions, or finding longer than average servo arms. Once set up on dual rates and exponential you have a model capable of taking the would be 3/4D flyer from tentative flying in the calm outdoors, to anything you can throw at it indoors. With a flying weight of 280gm (9-3/4oz) it was within the recommended specification and the power to weight ratio gives awesome performance.

Conclusions

Not the prettiest of biplanes, more like a cartoon figure, but does she perform! Excellent quality materials, plus a top class designer and very well executed Instruction Manual gives a package of high potential. Flying limitations are only from determined by the ability of the pilot.

Specification

Distributor	Helger Distribution
Wing Span	30in (760mm)
Weight	9.5oz (270gm)
Motor	370 Outrunner
Propeller	10 x 4.7in
Speed Controller	10amp brushless
Battery	Li-Po 7.4volt 860mAh
RRP	£39.99 (2006)

REVIEW - World Models Piper J-3 Cub 48

Surely one of the most popular scale ARTF models, the Piper Cub and Super Cub are available in a wide range of sizes for electric and IC power, World Models have no less than five different versions. A look at the proportions of the high wing Piper will give an immediate clue to the reasons for its popularity. It has the proportions of a good trainer/sports R/C model. Although normally destined for a 0.40 or 0.48 sized two, or four-stroke glow motor, I opted to fit a PAW 40 diesel for a change, diesel engines being noted for their ability to swing large diameter propellers at lower speeds. A bonus being that the silencer fitted more neatly within the cowling than that fitted to a glow motor of the same capacity.

At 71ins (1800mm) wing span the Piper Cub is quite a large model and you get a lot for your money. The package is very complete and includes the pre-built and covered airframe, GRP moulded cowling, plus all the necessary hardware and accessories. You have to supply the engine, propeller and radio. All the nuts, bolts, linkages etc. are bagged in groups, cross referred to the Instruction Manual for their deployment. Only open the bags as and when you need them, otherwise you will finish up with a multitude of small fixings with no certain ideas for their placement. Both the front windscreen and side windows are moulded, which makes the gluing and fitting much easier than if it were flat sheet. A separate clear cowling moulding enables you to cut and trim it for a good fit over the engine and silencer before tracing the cut-outs onto the GRP moulding proper.

The instructions rely on a pictorial approach, with line drawings and coded annotations telling you whether you have to cut, glue or screw and illustrating the fixings to use. No specific mention is made of the radio equipment requirements. The obvious minimum is a four-channel system with five servos (standard size) and the necessary extension and 'Y' leads. High wing models of the Piper Cub style can suffer from an effect where aileron control is given in one direction but the model yaws in the opposite direction. This is caused by the down going aileron creating excessive drag and negating the lift produced by the up going aileron. The problem can easily be corrected by introducing differential movement of the ailerons, limiting the amount of downward deflection. If you have a six-channel computer radio system the aileron servos can be plugged into separate channels and the differential movement programmed by the computer. If you only have a basic four-channel outfit the differential movement can be incorporated mechanically. This is done by moving the aileron horns back from the hinge line and by raking the servo arm forward, so that the effective movement of the rotary output is greater when moving the aileron upwards than it is in deflecting it downwards.

Watch out for

Joining the wing panels was very positive in location, the front fixing dowels are pre-fitted, but the rear reinforcing plywood plate has to be glued in position after the wing panels are joined, the holes for the wing bolts were incorrectly located. If, as quite often happens, the anchor nuts for the wings have not been pressed fully home you can cure the problem by positioning a piece of plywood across the fuselage at the rear wing

fixing location and having drilled holes where the wing bolts fit, tighten the bolts to pull the anchor nuts in position. Some epoxy should then be applied around the perimeter of the spiked anchor nuts.

All the control surface hinges are pre-fitted and secured and it is essential to fit the tailplane/ elevators and fin/rudder in the correct orders, this is not made absolutely clear in the instructions. A 1/4in packaging piece must first be removed from the end of the rear of the tailplane slot, the tailplane/elevators fitted, followed by the fin/ rudder. Dry fit the assemblies before final gluing and check the dimensions from the centre of the fuselage (on the former in front of the wing housing) to the tailplane tips to correctly locate the tailplane.

Some difficulty was experienced in trying to fit the rubber bung into the fuel tank. It was over large and the remedy was to use an abrasive tool to reduce the diameter of the bung. This can be done most conveniently if the bung, together with the metal plates, is fitted into a drill chuck before the pipes are installed and the assembly revolved and the tool applied to the bung.

Radio equipment layouts recommended work well, the route for the throttle linkage will vary from engine to engine and I used a long shank drill to go through the bulkhead and rear formers to give a direct connection from the engine carburettor to the throttle servo output. I would recommend not fitting the transparent windscreens until all of the radio equipment and linkages have been fitted, it is easier to get to the equipment in that way.

Wing struts are all pre-assembled and the nuts fitted to the wings for the fixing bolts. Precise dimensions are given for the location of the strut bolts in the wing are given in the instructions but if you look very closely at the covering it is possible to see where the bolts are inserted, use a pin to confirm the positions. If the struts are a touch short the holes in the aluminium strut ends can be elongated.

With the radio equipment installed as suggested the balance point was correct, you might have to fit the battery further forward if a lighter engine is used. Securing the aileron servos to the underside of the hatches does not allow much of the servo arm to protrude to the outer surface and you may have to connect the aileron pushrod to the outer servo arm holes. Even with the clevis fitted to the outmost hole on the control horn, too much movement on the aileron may be produced. If this movement cannot be reduced from the transmitter electronics you will have to enlarge the slot in the hatch so that the pushrod can be connected closer to the output centre.

Flight Characteristics

If you want to do some really scale flying the World Model Cub is for you, it is a tail-dragger and a high wing monoplane which means that you have to learn to co-ordinate rudder for take-off and with ailerons for balanced turns. However the co-ordination required is not difficult, you can mix rudder and aileron controls on the transmitter and the Cub is a very forgiving flyer unlikely to spring any surprises on you. Best of all it is very realistic in flight, it will execute all the manoeuvres of the full-size, which excludes extreme aerobatics, it is well behaved in the circuit and gives a very satisfying three point landing.

Conclusions

A well engineered kit, good value and would make an excellent introduction to scale modelling.

Specification

Wing Span	71in (1800mm)
Wing Area	698sq.in (45.0sq.dm)
Fuselage length	47in (1200mm)
Weight	5.5lb (2500gm)
Engine	0.40cu.in 2-stroke and 0.52cu.in 4-stroke
Radio Requires	4 channels 5 servos
Distributors	Steve Webb Models
Cost	£99.99(2006)

REVIEW - LN Model Vermont Belle 1300

Take a look at the Puffin Models advertisement for this model and you might be excused for thinking that this is a docile sports model. Lightly powered it could be a good second EP model, but with the full works of a brushless motor, the equivalent of a 0.30 or 0.40 IC motor and a three cell 3,400mAh Li-Po battery and you have a seriously aerobatic model. The generous control surfaces, lightweight structure, the total weight is only 1300gms (2lb 14oz) 3D flying becomes eminently possible.

Watch out for

For a successful highly aerobatic model you need a suitable design and a well-constructed airframe using quality materials, the Vermont Belle has these and the accessories are also of good quality and complete. Instructions leave a bit to be desired they are quite sparse, even for the experienced modeller. All the more reason, therefore, to take your time over the assembly, ensure that you understand the reasons for any action before taking it. The instructions may not be too explicit. Cut-outs for the mini servos at the rear of the fuselage are the same on both the left and right hand sides, this gives you the option of using one servo for each of the elevators and dispensing with the wire elevator joiner. Note that the tailplane extends to the fuselage sternpost and no infill piece is required, as suggested in the instructions. The separated control surfaces are hinged using the special clear tape supplied. You may find that the leading edges of the ailerons are slightly bowed, this is not critical but after top hinging I would recommend doubling back the control surface and applying another layer of tape on the inside surfaces, this will not affect the freedom of the hinge.

The hole for the front wing dowel is pre-formed in the former, but requires opening up in the reinforcing behind the former. Adequately reinforce the rear wing mounting plate with hard balsa on either side of the plate to sandwich it firmly in position. Epoxy the anchor nuts to the plate. Reinforcing the front bulkhead is also a wise precaution if you are using a powerful motor, epoxy some 1/4in(6mm) triangular strips at the rear of the bulkhead. Pieces of 1.5mm plywood behind the balsawood sheeting will strengthen the servo screw fixings for the ailerons and a touch of cyano stiffens the screw holes for the elevator and rudder servo screws.

A three piece Liteply battery tray is supplied, but no indication of the precise location in the fuselage. The accompanying photograph should help in this respect, the front should leave sufficient room for the motor and ESC and connectors. It is essential to secure the battery adequately, use Velcro pads and straps. The pianowire leg for the tailwheel is very light gauge, probably the best method of securing it is to bend a right angle at the top, insert it into the rudder and bind and epoxy it to the rudder leading edge. The fitting of the canopy was left until last, it is a thin moulding and could be easily damaged. Trim below the lower trim lines otherwise the overlap onto the fuselage is minimal.

Flight Qualities

With the battery positioned well forward the balance point was 4in (100mm) behind the wing leading edge, well within the prescribed limits. Take-off is accomplished in a matter of feet, at

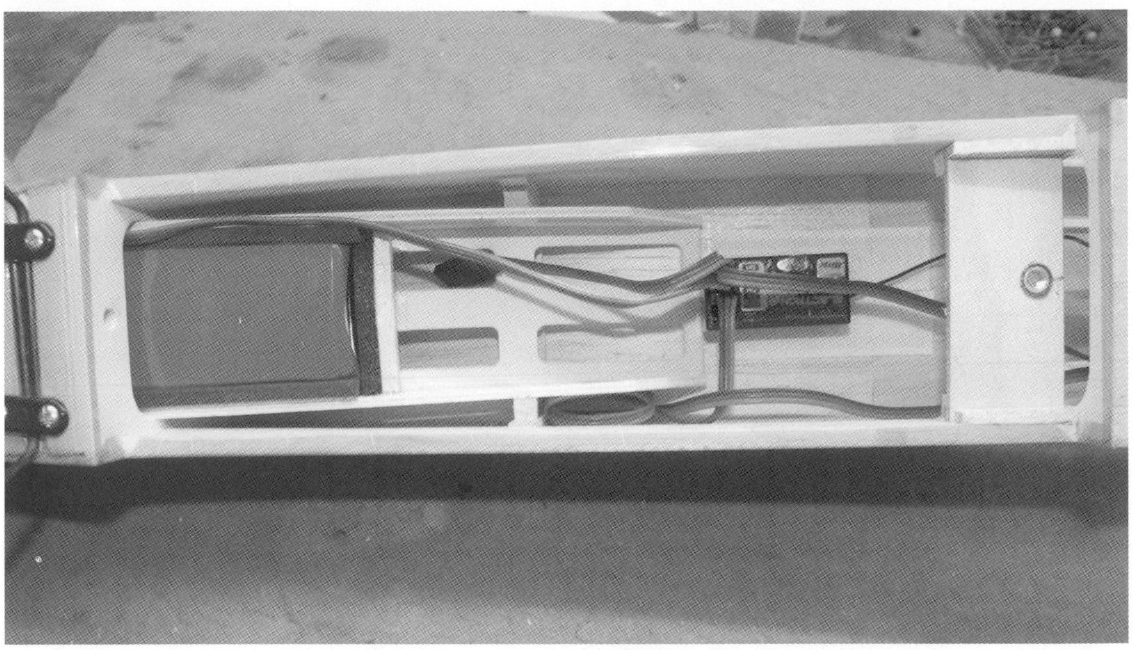

considerably less than full power and the Vermont Belle climbs quickly away like a home-sick angel. With the recommended power train there is more than ample power for all of the accepted 3D manoeuvres of the prop-hanging type, the roll rate is very rapid and radii of looping manoeuvres very tight. Slow speed is impeccable, the stalling speed being very low and the ailerons being responsive all the way. Instructions state that as much rudder movement as possible should be arranged, this is correct and even with the movement limited by the elevators you still need more for knife-edge looping.

Conclusions

A very adaptable model capable of a wide-ranging performance. Use exponential control and limited movements for learning and then increase the movements for a wow-and-a-half experience. With the installations as described the flight time is very generous.

Specifications

Supplier :Puffin Models Ltd., Unit D3 Backfield Farm Rural Business Park, Wotton Road, Iron Acton, Bristol BS37 9X9 (01454 228184)

Wing Span	1300mm (51ins)
Length	1100mm (43ins)
Weight	2lbs 14oz (1300gms) actual
Motor	Mega 22/30/3E brushless
ESC	Jeti 40
Battery	11.1volt 3400mAh LiPo
Price	£114.95 (2006)

REVIEW - Ripmax Bosanova

Cute lines, an attractive decorative scheme and an air of purposeful flyability sums up the first impressions of the Bosanova. It is marketed as a 3D machine capable of extreme manoeuvres and while this may be true it doesn't have the fragile looks of some of the extreme machines and look as though it would fall apart if landed too heavily. Indeed, with lower power and control movements it would make a good aerobatic trainer. It is a kit with a relatively small number of structural components, including a one piece, five feet span wing, making for a fairly rapid build. Because the film covering involves the decorative film being applied over the base film you must take care when cutting out for servo fitting etc. and you may need to fuelproof the edges of such items as the underwing stars to prevent them lifting when the fuel gets to them.

Kit contents are both comprehensive and fit for their purpose, the only exception to this was the undercarriage fixing on early kits. The distributors have addressed this problem with a modification and addendum sheet. The full colour instruction manual is well illustrated and written in sound English; if anything it is a little too polite in some areas, were it states 'You may wish to' or 'it is a good idea to' - just do it.

Watch out for

Following the order of assembly recommended in the manual will have you fitting the cockpit canopy at an early stage; a big no-no as it will probably be damaged during the remainder of the

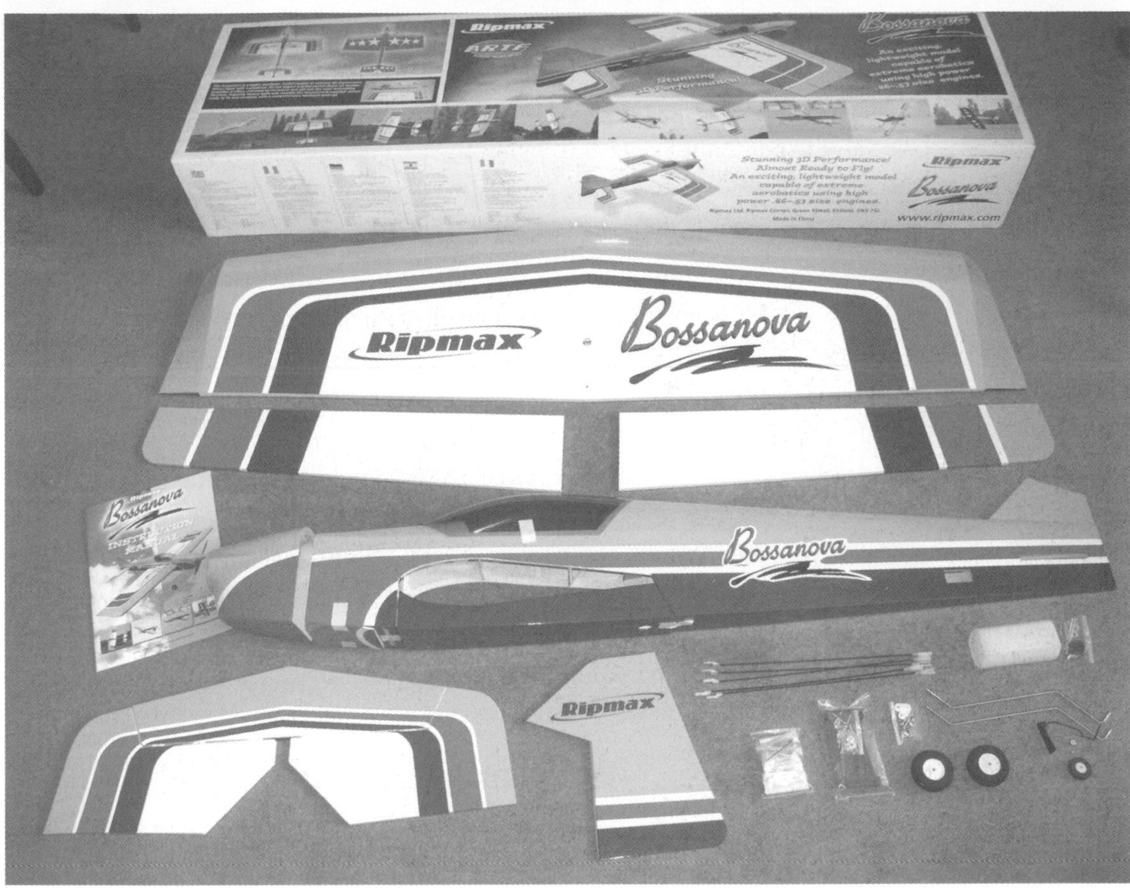

assembly. I also prefer to fit the engine and cowling before the tail surfaces and the control horns before gluing the tail surfaces into position. Not for the first time in an imported ARTF kit the dimension for the engine prop-driver to the engine bulkhead was wrongly quoted, it should be at a minimum of 130mm and a touch more if you are using a spinner with a recessed rear skirt. Centre lines on the engine bulkhead were only faintly marked, emphasise these with a ballpoint pen before attempting to position the engine bearers. When the engine mount fixing-bolt holes have been marked and punched on the bulkhead, drill 4.5mm holes and fit the spiked anchor nuts to the rear, you will need some long nose pliers or forceps to locate them. Using a large diameter 'penny' washer under the bolt head tighten until the anchor nut is securely dug into the rear of the bulkhead, then further secure with epoxy.

Radio installations present no real problems, but you will need five servo extension leads, approximately 300mm long, to connect the aileron servos and the elevator and rudder servos situated at the rear of the fuselage, plus a 'Y' lead. The fuselage is quite shallow at the location of the receiver, but there is just enough room to have the receiver protected by a sheath of foam rubber. With a four or five cell 800mAh battery located under the fuel tank the balance point should be spot on.

Flight Characteristics

With the Irvine 53 two-stroke engine fitted the

pressure nipple on the silencer was hard up against the cowling, making it difficult to remove the tubing when filling the fuel tank. One option was to close the needle valve to prevent flooding the engine; the other was to put the model on a wing tip so that the fuel would pour out of the silencer as soon as the tank was full. A neater answer might be to fit a refuelling valve, although that may make the removal and refitting of the cowling more difficult.

Initial flights were carried out with a slightly forward balance point and limited control movements - no mock-heroics at this stage - and the take-off was commendably straight, with lift-off occurring with a small application of up elevator. A touch of up elevator and right aileron trim had the Bosanova flying straight and level and the straight tracking continued through the looping manoeuvres, which had commendably small radii considering the limited movements and forward balance point. In slow flight the model was very stable, even in turbulent air conditions. The landing approach was easy and predictable, again reinforcing thoughts of it being used in a trainer mode, and apart from the failure of the undercarriage (later modified) the initial impressions were very good. Further outings with increased control movements confirmed the aerobatic performance of the Bosanova, including 3D manoeuvres and prop-hanging; it may not be quite as agile as some of the smaller, or very lightweight 3D models, but it has the potential to satisfy the trainee for this style of flying.

Conclusions

Larger than many 3D models, the Bosanova has a wide range of flight characteristics and is certainly easier to see than its smaller brethren. A good choice for anyone wishing to try some of the more advanced aerobatic manoeuvres - or, with lower power, basic aerobatics before advancing further. Remember that powered by an engine at the top of the range it is a potent machine and could be over-stressed if full power is used in extended dives etc., full throttle is there only for vertical and high drag manoeuvres, not as a 'slam open and leave it there' instrument.

Specifications

Distributor	Ripmax Ltd.
Wing span	60ins (1520mm)
Engine	.46 - .53 two-stroke, .52 - .70 four-stroke
Weight	2300g approx. (4lb 9oz)
Radio	4 channel
Servos	5 standard size
RRP	£129.99 (2006)

REVIEW - Cermark New Timer EP

Vintage style models have a popular following with enthusiasts looking for more relaxed flying combined with the elegance and character of designs from yesteryear. Vintage does not, however, mean old fashioned cut and glue construction methods. A new generation of models combine modern materials, ARTF techniques and offer a rapid 'from opening the kit box, to flying' time. Cermark's New Timer is based on the pylon models of 50 years ago, but features two important changes. Electric power takes over from IC engines and the fuselage is a smart GRP moulding - it is also radio controlled. High quality prefabrication, the Speed 480 motor is pre-fitted, together with a spun aluminium spinner. The flying surfaces are all from balsawood with excellent Ultracote covering and the undercarriage is ready for screwing in place. Instructions are adequate, but with limited illustrations. Better indications of the locations of the servos would make life easier for newcomers and the New Timer could be then classed as a beginners model.

Watch out for

There is a minimum of assembly work with this kit; the two wing panels aligned accurately and the dihedral brace didn't require any trimming. The wings are banded onto the fuselage pylon and because the GRP pylon moulding and the film-covered wing are smooth, shiny surfaces there is a risk that the wing will easily be displaced from its seating. To prevent this happening thin foam wing seating tape strips should be attached to the edges of the pylon top surface. Level the fuselage moulding where the tailplane sits as there is

inevitably a ridge where the fuselage moulded halves are joined and this must be removed for the tailplane to sit level.

The manual suggests that the mass of wires should keep the battery and ESC in position, I opted to fix the receiver to the inner wall of the fuselage with double-sided tape. Do not wrap the battery and ESC in protective foam, you must allow for the cooling air to pass over them to exit at the fuselage outlets at the rear wing location. Take the receiver aerial through a hole in the underside of the fuselage and route it to the rear tailskid, it's neater than using an air exit opening.

Flight Characteristics

The New Timer flew out steadily in a stately manner from a hand launch, giving immediate confidence. A good climb rate takes her effortlessly to a couple of hundred feet at which height the motor can be cut and the model put into glide mode. There is very little trim change required on the transition from power to glide and the control responses remain positive on the glide. It was easy to line-up the model for a landing approach but, due to the excellent glide performance, it is easy to overshoot the landing; a dab of up elevator gives the required round out for a soft touch down. Turns are well co-ordinated, with no loss of height under power and flying control is strictly non-frenetic.

Conclusions

This polyhedral wing pseudo-vintage model has both elegance and efficiency, with the power package recommended there is ample power to climb to height, glide, find thermals and have consistent flights of 20 minutes or more. With the proviso of a limited amount of instruction from an experienced flyer in the first instance, the New Timer can be recommended as a beginners model. Installing an eight-cell battery pack and a 7x5ins propeller, but retaining the standard motor, will improve the aerobatic performance and loops and rolls are easily performed. However, the New Timer is essentially for relaxed flying in true vintage style, it does it with beauty and grace.

Specifications

Distributor	CML Distribution
Wing Span	56in
Weight	23oz (630gm)
Motor	Speed 480 direct drive (supplied)
Propeller	7x3ins (supplied)
Radio	3 Channel minimum, with 2 micro servos
ESC	Cermark SC-20, or equivalent
Battery	7 cell NiMh 800 to 1200 mAh
RRP	£79.99 (2006)

REVIEW - V-MAR Stinger - with floats

Floats and Floatplanes have been rather ignored by the ARTF manufacturers but this has been rectified by a couple of companies, one of them being V-MAR. Designed for models in the general range of models with a total weight, including floats, of 5 to 9lbs (2200 to 4000gms) and 0.40 to 0.60 power the floats are balsawood framed, foam filled and covered with pre-decorated Polycote film. The hard points for fixing the struts, spacers and hardware are supplied in the kit. Alternative water rudders, from an extended air rudder or fixed to the rear of one float, are also included.

You would probably fit a 0.40 size engine in the 63in span, high wing Stinger for training purposes on the land, but for operating off water the V-MAR 52 was installed. With a semi-symmetrical section wing the Stinger makes a good all-weather (well, most weathers) trainer, it is of conventional design and traditional wood construction. The covering is colourful and the overall effect of the Stinger on the V-MAR floats is most attractive. Kit contents are very complete and include fuel tank, wheels and spinner. By using the float rudder and closed loop control it would be possible to make the model convertible to land or water flying.

Watch out for

If you intend to fly the Stinger off water you should make the model as watertight as possible to prevent water getting to the internals of the airframe when the model is accidentally 'dunked'. Use silicone sealant when fixing the float attachment and around the fuel tank neck and any external screws; give the engine bay an extra coat of fuel proofer and use wing-seating tape for the wing to fuselage seating. Ensure that the edges of the covering are secure, fuelproof if necessary, particularly on the floats.

Improvements have resulted in a three pipe fuel tank being included and the engine is now bolted direct to the engine bearers, so ignore the manual in these respects. Also, the wheels, nose leg and steering arm are pre-fitted. Check the servo arm connectors, they may not have long enough threaded screws to extend through some thicker arms and it may be necessary to drill out the holes in the control horns. Note that the direction of rudder control movement shown in the manual is - or was - incorrect. No dimension is quoted for the length of the water rudder extension, 6in (155mm) from the underside of the air rudder to the bottom of the water rudder is about right.

Flight Characteristics

The 'Stinger' handles well on the water, using the extended water rudder, operating from the air rudder via a piano-wire rod. It may not be the most elegant solution, but it is effective. Although it is stable on the water you should take care when taxiing crosswind, it is a high wing model and a strong gust could tip it over. Once in position for the take-off run, reduce the throttle and the model will automatically weathercock into wind. Gradually increase the power and the 'Stinger' will rise onto the step (the front portion of the floats) quite quickly and it continues to track straight into wind, requiring very little rudder correction. Once flying speed has been reached a touch of up elevator will lift her clear off the water, the up elevator should then be removed; in the air she handles smoothly but, with the extra lateral area of the floats you will find that the co-ordination of rudder and ailerons, plus an input of elevator, is required for continued banked turns. Touchdowns on water are not traumatic, the model is best flown onto the surface at just above the stalling speed and when you achieve this there is a special feeling of satisfaction.

Conclusion

In its land form it is a sensibly sized economic trainer having the advantage of a semi-symmetrical wing section. The kit, with a very few minor exceptions, assembles easily and rapidly and a standard four to six channel radio and a 0.40 size engine will complete the package. For waterplane flying you will need to increase the engine size, the floats are ideal for the Stinger and they are also suitable for a wide variety of other models.

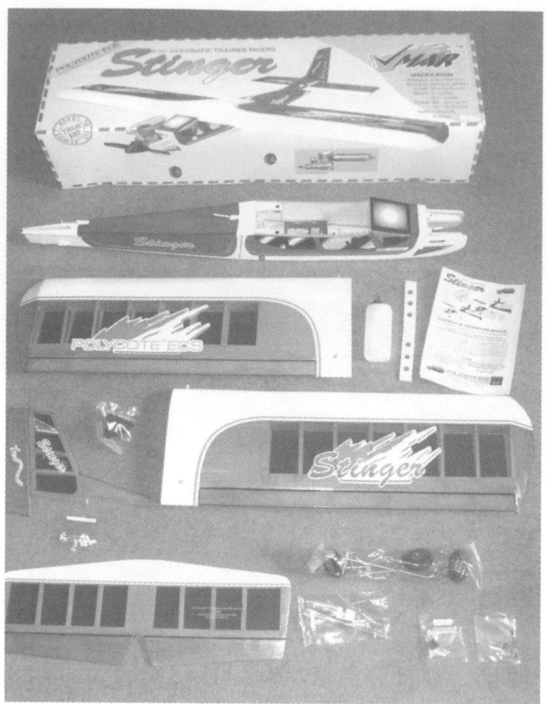

Specifications

Distributor	MacGregor Industries
Wing span	63-1/4in (1607mm)
Wing area	730sq.in
Engine range	0.40 – 0.52cu.in (2 stroke)
	0.48 - 56cu.ins. (4 stroke)
Control functions	Ailerons, elevator, rudder and throttle
Weight	5.5 - 6.2lb
RRP	£64.95 (2006)

V-MAR Floats

For most 0.40 to 0/60 powered models

Length	32in (813mm)
RRP	£44.95 (2006)